SUBJECT **THE LAW OF THE PLAYGROUND**

NAME Jonathan Blyth

with sarah morgan
and phil Gianville

for mark Hearn

SUBJECT THE LAW OF THE PLAYGROUND

NAME Jonathan Blyth

with Sarah Morgan
and Phil Gianville

A puerile and Disturbing
dictionary of playground
insults and games

EBURY
PRESS

First published in Great Britain in 2004

10 9 8 7 6 5 4

Text © Jonathan Blyth 2004

Jonathan Blyth has asserted his right to be identified as the author of this work
under the Copyright, Designs and Patents Act 1988.

First published by
Ebury Press
Random House, 20 Vauxhall Bridge Road, London SW1V 2SA

Random House Australia (Pty) Limited
20 Alfred Street, Milsons Point, Sydney, New South Wales 2061, Australia

Random House New Zealand Limited
18 Poland Road, Glenfield, Auckland 10, New Zealand

Random House South Africa (Pty) Limited
Endulini, 5A Jubilee Road, Parktown 2193, South Africa

The Random House Group Limited Reg. No. 954009

www.randomhouse.co.uk

A CIP catalogue record for this book is available from the British Library.

Cover designed by seagulls
Text design and typesetting by seagulls

ISBN 0091900301

Printed and bound in Great Britain by Mackays of Chatham

Papers used by Ebury Press are natural, recyclable products made
from wood grown in sustainable forests.

Foreword

In 1999, after an orgy of nostalgia with a few old school friends, I thought to myself I must have gone to the strangest school in England. The strange kids seemed particularly strange and the bullies seemed unusually inventive. To prove it, I wrote up as many memories as I could muster, and put them on the Internet. I included an invitation for readers to share their own stories.

The trickle, flow, then flood of emails I received put me squarely in my place. My childhood was somewhere between tame and mundane.

The site took off with disparate responses; I received emails from 15 year olds with axes to grind: *'THERE IS A FAT GIRL IN OUR CLSAS WE THRO CHAIRS AT HER AN SHE CRIES BUT SHE IS SO FAT SHE DESERVES IT HA HA KELLY YOU FAT BITCH.'* On the day this arrived, I got a message from a 50-year-old woman who shared with us the trauma of developing oversized breasts as a pre-teen in 1960s America. It was a mixed crowd.

Often, bullies shared their experiences by way of shame-faced apology. Very often, the bullied shared their experiences by way of — occasionally explosive — catharsis. You may have seen those entries on Friends Reunited: *'I'm getting married to the East Midlands' Area Manager for Tesco, and what are you doing, eh? You're nothing, Tony. And you've got a tiny cock, and I've done your dad.'*

FOREWORD

I didn't put these entries up on the site, for two reasons. One, in case Tony's cock was reading and feeling litigious, and the real reason ... it just wasn't really that funny. Unless you get your kicks poking swords into car crashes, to see if anything screams.

As many times as I've tried to distil a philosophy for the website – and consequently this book – it boils down to only three things. It had to be funny, it had to be true (or a really cool lie) and it had to be something a little less workaday than the rules to British Bulldog. If you don't already know those, you're not really missing anything.

WHAT THIS BOOK ISN'T, THEN WHAT IT IS

This isn't a comprehensive list of insults, slang, and the name of that frog who liked milkshakes in *Bod*. You won't find the rules to every game you used to play in this dictionary.

Do you remember that skipping game? Bumper car, bumper car, number 28? Yeah, so do I, and I'm a boy. But I much prefer the version where the amount of skips corresponds to the number of dollops of poo there is in that girl's knickers.

Fundamentally, this book is a testimony and a tribute to how clever, inspired, unpleasant, stupid, heartbreaking, evil and childish children have been, and still are. But, you know, not in a patronising way.

THINGS THAT MAY MAKE YOU RAISE AN EYEBROW

The inventiveness of children is famously unconstrained by the considerations that dog us as adults. Any misty-eyed fool can tell you that. So imaginations are freer, trains of thought derail more easily, and ... boundaries are less respected.

What I'm edging towards saying is that children (apart from some girls, and that bookish boy who uses the word 'actually' too often) are not great respecters of political correctness. They're flippantly racist, often lacking in empathy, disrespectful of religious differences, homophobic, and they're not desperately diplomatic around the fat and the disabled, either.

And yet, it's funny. Perhaps because we've so painstakingly learned to be horrified by these things, so it's jarring and funny to hear them spouted by someone else. It also gives us the rewarding chance to show our horror, and to prove to everyone around us that *we* wouldn't talk like that, God no.

But it's also funny because there's often a charming lack of genuine malice in certain insults. Take 'gay'. Gay now means 'rubbish'. How can you be outraged by someone calling your trainers gay?

As grown-up, intelligent people, of course, we know that using gay as a generic insult creates a powerful sense that gayness is, of itself, a bad thing. And that undoubtedly causes some children of wavering sexuality (and that fusty-jacketed English lit. teacher) some distress. But to put your hands over your ears and deny that children can be obnoxious, thoughtless, flippantly racist and homophobic is stupid; and to deny that it's often done in a way that is startlingly funny is, frankly, your loss.

We have, however, endeavoured to straddle a line which recognises the invention but doesn't wallow in the malice. But they deserve to be remembered; a lot of the stories in this book are, after all, the reason we're all so brilliantly fucked up today.

By the way, the name of the frog in *Bod* was Alberto.

JONATHAN BLYTH
London, 2004

NUMBERS

10 print 'hello', 20 goto 10 If you're not aware of this, the simplest of BASIC programs, then you were possibly good at football. Variations were many, but primarily involved replacing 'hello' with 'fuck you'. You could also add a semi-colon after the closing speech marks, which as *everyone* knows means that the whole screen will become a mad blur of profanity. Or 'hello'.

If you don't want to tell anyone to fuck off, simply use the opportunity to tell everyone how big and hairy your willy is.

3d ride Upstairs on a double-decker bus, take the seat at the very front on the right-hand side. The impact of any low-hanging branches against the front windscreen will create the impression of an exciting 3D simulator, and the thirteen or so children crammed into the 'best seat on the ride' will scream '3D RIDE!' as they tumble happily to the floor.
See also: bus tipping

3d6 If you were into role-playing games, this was shorthand for the rolling of three six-sided dice, used to generate a number between 3 and 18. This roll is used to generate the 'stats' of your Dark Elf, or Halfling, so you can tell whether he will be able to be really strong, like you aren't.

On no account did you use this term in the real world, knowing that the little lead goblins that you had painted so lovingly would get thrown out of the window.

7 minutes The amount of time it takes to smoke a cigarette without undue *bumming* and get to a class. 'Have you got seven minutes?' was therefore a coded invitation for a cigarette.

A a

abc 1. US; a mild term to describe a piece of chewing gum that has *already been chewed*. **2.** UK; you would be asked, 'Are you ABC?' If you replied no, then your interrogator would look shocked and say, 'What, you're not *a brilliant child*?' If you answered yes, then you are an *African Bum Cleaner*.

African Bum Cleaners were often required for those who suffered from *skil*. **See also: skil**

actually, my mum's in a wheelchair

A one-off defence to a parental insult. Alternatively, your father might be dead. Generally, this will result in a shocked apology from the insulter, giving you the opportunity to laugh in their face.

Warning: This defence only works against children who *give a shit*. The more deranged or sociopathic children may say 'Good', or 'So's my dad, and he's fucking your mum in hell, and she's going oo, oo, harder'.

adidas

Apart from being a brand of sportswear, Adidas also stands for a number of things, the most well-known being '*all day I dream about sex*'. However, there are others:

'after dinner I do a shit'

'a dick is dirty after sex'
'a Durex is disposable after sex'
'a dildo inserted deeply
adds stimulation'
'after diarrhoea, I detest anal sex'
For double Adidas, try:
'after dinner I did a shit and did it
down a sewer'
And finally, the old forwards–backwards:
'after dinner I did a shit,
soon after dessert I did another'
Unsurprisingly, the only phrase to have been used as the title of a popular song is 'All Day I Dream About Sex', by Outkast and Killer Mike.

ah, condor

Said after a fart, after taking in a deep breath and looking deeply satisfied. Based on an old advert for Condor pipe tobacco, a tobacco which will surely die out as the schoolchildren of yesterday – tomorrow's pipe smokers – think, 'Ooh, I bet that smells of farts.'

aids

A disease that is surprisingly easy to diagnose. Tell the patient to hold their breath, then inform them that they can breathe out *'if they have AIDS'*. As long as they never breathe out, they've got the all-clear.

ambassadors for the school

'Remember now, you're ambassadors for the school, so *no loutish behaviour.'*

A phrase used to any group of schoolchildren as they got off the tatty hire coach. This was laughably designed to appeal to a sense of school loyalty, and inspire pride in the sudden trust that the school had put in you. You were *ambassadors!*

One week later, zookeepers in Chessington would phone the school and say, 'Hello? Ravensbourne School for Boys? You sent a busload of your ambassadors around, and they covered our lions in lager.'

ambush!

A variation on 'tag', *Ambush!* required only one intentional player. Everyone else was simply unaware that they were playing. The person who was 'it' had to sneak up behind someone and push them to the ground.

What distinguished this from a common or garden violent assault and transformed it into the fun game *Ambush!* was the fact you shouted 'AMBUSH!'

american holidays

Before everyone hated America, any child going on holiday to the States would return with amazing stories of having seen *Jaws 5*, buying Nike Air Max 9 trainers, '*which are actually called sneakers you know*', and playing Super Mario 7 on the Giga Nintendo.

If challenged to bring in these artefacts, acceptable excuses included 'they were taken off me at customs', 'they're at my gran's house', or 'you're not ready for them yet'.

and-a-roo

A game to be played with a consenting Andrew. A line of players take it in turns to slap Andrew, poke his face, or otherwise goad him. At random intervals, the hitherto placid Andrew should unleash a severe kicking to his antagonists, after which Andrew 'resets', and the game starts again.

Based on the game Buckaroo, which features a grumpy plastic mule.

animal farm

A film so famous and so largely unseen that it borders on urban legend. In it, a man makes sweet love to a chicken, and a woman shares that most intimate pleasure with a horse.

The closest most children would get to this film would be a surge of 200 tit-thirsty teenagers invading Dave's house, having gained wind of a seventh-generation copy belonging to Dave's older brother. He had, of course, lent it out.

Nowadays children have fingertip access to pictures of men having sex with sombreros. Pornography is no longer sacred.

any dream will do

A song from the godawful *Joseph and the Amazing Technicolor Dreamcoat*, and quite easily changed to 'I Did A Huge Poo'. One extended form includes:

I closed my eyes (I closed my eyes)
Walked into a table (ah-a aah)
Now I'm disabled (aah aah)

The song then kind of just stops, the thinking *probably* being that disabled people can't sing songs. Of course, you can simply change the second line from 'drew back the curtains' to 'drew back my foreskin', then mime wanking for the remainder of the lunch hour. Alternatively, sing this slightly more thought-out version:

I closed my eyes,
drew back my foreskin,
To see for certain,
what I thought I knew.
There was a yeast,
the skin was breaking,
My bell-end's aching, any cream'll do.

apaches The name of a safety awareness film in which children die in stupid ways, so you don't have to. One film featured a mother selfishly making dinner as her unsupervised children cheerfully drank weedkiller, drowned in silage and threw themselves at tractors.

There was another film set in a building site, which featured a shoe with a bit of foot in it.

appetite for cheeky bum sex A less-macho name for Guns n' Roses' multi-million selling album, *Appetite for Destruction*.

are you a benny tied to a tree? Ask someone whether they are a benny tied to a tree. After a moment's thought, their response will generally be 'no'. Because they're obviously not, you see? This gives you the opportunity to run away, screaming at the top of your voice, 'BENNY ON THE LOOSE!'

are you a comedian? Poor question for a teacher to ask of the class clown. If the child replies yes, the teacher is forced to either tell the child to leave the class, or invite him to 'entertain us, then'. If the child truly succeeds in entertaining the class, of course, he will be sent from the classroom to smoke in the corridor.

arranged marriage 'Step on a crack, you break your back; step on a line, you break your spine.'

A rhyme for girls. Once proclaimed, any girl stepping on a crack or line would be forever doomed to the vague threat of a broken back. The lack of a scheduled time for the tragedy was the only comfort.

A lesser-known rhyme threatened the girl with this dread fate:

Step on a nick,
you marry a brick,
and a beetle will come to
your wedding.

A nick and a line being arguably similar, it was interesting how many girls argued that what they had stepped on was a line, opting for lifelong paralysis over a poorly attended wedding to a brick.

arrows An illustrative device designed to bring a poor drawing (usually of a classmate eating a poo) back into the grounds of recognisability. *See illustrations.*

Lesson 1: Basics
Note that in the left drawing, it is clear that James is the focus of the gayness. In the diagram on the right, it could be simply that James has gay lips, and doesn't fancy boys at all. There is no right and wrong; just consider what you are trying to say.

Lesson 2: Beyond Arrows

On the left, we have the simple but pleasing idea that Simon eats poo from a wooden spoon. However, the speech bubble makes it clear that Simon loves and demands his ration of bumbrown, and the title shows that this is a daily occurence at Simon's house, as his family cannot even afford Blue Riband biscuits.

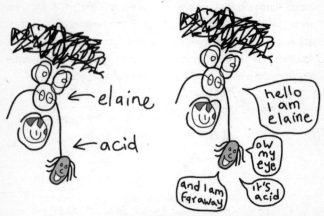

Lesson 3: Damage Limitation

What is going on in the left drawing? It is difficult to tell. The arrows let us know that Elaine is snotting acid, but it is on the right that we see the full story: the snot is going into the victim's *eye* – despite the snotline not actually reaching the eye – and the reason the head is so small is that it is a long way away. Demonstrating Elaine's filthy ability to fling snot long distance, and backwards.

Arrrrrrrr A phrase designed to 'put the willies up' someone who has broken the rules. In cases of extreme naughtiness, you should add details of the misdemeanour and as much information about the wrongdoer as possible. For instance ...

'Arrrrrrrr, Jonathan Blyth, Form 2C1, 150 Walsingham Road, Nottingham, England, The World, we saw you sniffing glluuuuueeee.'

Regional variations include 'aaaaaahhh' (West Country), 'ummmmm' (Lincolnshire), 'errrrrr' (Midlands), 'eeehhhh' (North East). But the finest variation is the 'Just You Wait, Cha-Cha-Cha', which involves repeating the phrase 'Just You Wait, Cha-Cha-Cha' and shaking a pair of invisible maracas until the wrongdoer bursts into tears.

assembly safari 'When the drama workshop put on a production called *African Jigsaw*, part of their show was the creation of eerily realistic zebras' heads out of papier mâché. It was fairly common for these curious beasts to make an appearance in assemblies, poking their heads inquisitively from behind the stage curtains, looking around a bit to see what was going on, then disappearing. It wasn't unlike a Morecambe & Wise Christmas Special.'

B b

bananas? A cutting, sarcastic put-down used by a maths teacher when a pupil answers a question without stating the units. In action:

TEACHER: What's the volume of a cube with sides of 2cm each?

PUPIL: Eight.

TEACHER: Eight what? Bananas?

Pupils would then fall out of their chairs and asphyxiate with laughter. Also accepted amongst teachers as an *inherently funny thing* are elephants. So, also consider, 'Eight what? Elephants?'

A further alternative allows the teacher to prove how clever he is with a gleeful pun:

PUPIL: Sixteen.

TEACHER: You nit!

Ha ha, sir. Ha.

bang bang, you're dead, 50 bullets in your head A threat. The number would rise to increase the severity of the threat. Claims of a million or even infinity bullets were not rare. If you found you had an extra few seconds after shooting your victim in the head, you could offer them a little more information about the bullets you shot them with:

One's black, one's blue,
one full of chicken poo

or:
One red, one blue,
one made of doggie poo

We see here that the colour of the first bullet is flexible, as is the animal what did the poo.

bangkok An educational form of violence. A boy is asked the capital of Thailand, and before really giving him a genuine chance to answer, the questioner shouts 'BANG COCK!' and punches him in the downbelows.

barker '95 challenge Based on the Pepsi Challenge. Participants are offered one cup of squash diluted with tap water, and one cup of squash diluted with – ideally – river water that has just trickled through the corpse of a sheep.

They are then offered the chance to say which is the real 'Barker '95'. Their answer is entirely irrelevant.

baron fishponds Baron, in the 80s, were a brand of shoes so under-spokenly unfashionable that they were nearly outside the bullying radar. *Nearly*. The stitching on the top formed a kind of lip, which would hold water in the rain. Thus, Baron Fishponds, an unpopular and well-kicked aristocrat, was born.

barry, the name of heroes The name Barry seems inseparable from idiocy – perhaps because any parent choosing the name Barry must be incapable of teaching their son basic motor skills, let alone higher brain function. Here are but a few examples of UK Barries flying their colours:

'When asked if his name was Barry, our Barry replied "Yes". The teacher replies "Yes what?", quite naturally expecting him to answer "Yes, Miss". However, our Barry replied, after some thought, "Yes ... please?" The word "please" was drawn out in a slightly puzzled tone of voice, which would have been heartbreaking if it wasn't so funny.'

'Excited by the joke, "Knock Knock/ Who's there?/Spitonmish/Spitonmish

Who?", in his first telling, Barry blurted the whole thing out, including the cue for the other person to spit on his shoe. In a rare moment of befuddled pity, Barry's victim passed up the opportunity to spit on Barry's shoe, shook his head sadly and walked off. Barry was unable to work out exactly what he'd done wrong.'

'Barry did a cracking and voluntary impression of the Pink Panther walking into a tree. It wasn't an accident; it was an impression. I hope this has stood him in good stead throughout his life, as it seemed to be his only skill.'

bastard week An impromptu celebration, lasting one week, during which pupils partook in the following activities:

- knee kicking
- gobbing in hoods
- throwing people down the stairs
- slashing of the neck with metal combs, and
- surprise karate chops to the Adam's apple 10 seconds before a teacher entered the class; this resulted in a

complete inability to breathe, so the recipient wouldn't be able to answer the register. Which would obviously be his number one concern, what with not being able to breathe.

Warning: Karate chops to the neck actually DO result in the complete inability to breathe.

batiment French word for *building*; also amusingly sounds like the West Indian slang for homosexual, *batty man*. If you are taking German instead of French, you aren't without fun gay words: the German word for ambassador is *Botschafter*.

b.c.g. The mandatory inoculation against tuberculosis, that all children without a natural immunity had to take. The test for this immunity was a hexagon of pin-pricks in the forearm, which became red and slightly inflamed if you were already immune. Basically, an inflamed forearm meant you didn't get the needle.

Attempts to avoid the jab by simulating this effect were common by stabbing yourself with a dirty compass. One reported child, however, excelled in this field by savaging his arm with an arsenal of pencils, drawing pins and fingernails, until his forearm was not so much inflamed, more gaping and infected.

The nurse wasn't convinced with the child's explanations that this simply meant that he was super-immune, and that his massive trauma was the product of really kick-ass antibodies.

beats Game played with two teams of four or five. One team would pick a password or phrase, and then peg it. The other team would hunt down the opposing individuals, catch them and beat the password – and shit – out of them. Two matching passwords from two (usually badly hurt) individuals, and the game was won.

Often phrases like 'fuck your mum' were chosen by the running team – knowing that the weakest members of the team would get caught first. The only way they would therefore be able to stop the beating was by shouting

'fuck your mum' at the attackers, which obviously sounded more like a spirited defiance, and left the victim five times likelier to get their nose broken.
See also: catch 22; heats

beebusters! A game/pastime for seven year olds, based loosely on the *Ghostbusters* phenomenon. First, up to four participants found a girl and dragged her to a section of the field where there was a bumble bee. The girl would become scared. Sensing that fear, the gang of *Beebusters* would shout '*Beebusters!*' and jump with both feet around the rough area of the alleged bee.

Having been saved from the bumble menace, the girl was then allowed to go back to doing handstands against a wall.

bender card An imaginary card that you never knew you had until you were informed that you had dropped it. An instinctive glance at the ground is then instant proof that you must belong to this exclusive club – otherwise, why are you looking for your membership card?

Reversible if you picked up the imaginary card and said, 'There must be some mistake, this is your card. It's even got a little picture of you bumming your dad.'

Similarly, any response to a cry of 'Oi, you've dropped your lipstick' would be enough to prove your gayness. But not for girls, obviously.

betty swollocks and friends
Spoonerism-based names used when a supply teacher takes the class. Includes, but is by no means limited to: Betty Swollocks, Paul Smeenis, Mary Hinge, Kelly Smunt, Joe Blobb, Tex Soy, Trevor Nyeanalsecks, and the virtually unspottable (if slightly flawed) Keith Burton.

Not to be confused with the less sophisticated Bart Simpson-esque humour of names like Mike Hunt, Hugh Jarse, etc.

be-yourselves, the
An early example of girls being more emotionally and psychologically advanced than boys.

'A group was started in our school called "The Freds", a club for boys in which every member adopted the name Fred. A rival gang was started up to challenge The Freds, in which everyone was called Herman. They weren't quite as cool as The Freds, but they tried hard.

'Piqued by their exclusion from such groups, the girls decided to counter with "The Be-Yourselves", a gang in which members proudly went by … their own name. Presumably, this was accompanied by some Care-Bears-grade sentiment about how pretending to be something you're not will only end in sadness and boo-hoos.

'The respect accorded to The Be-Yourselves was demonstrated graphically by a guy bringing up a bunch of snot on to a piece of paper, writing "The Be-Yourselves" with an arrow pointing to it, and showing it to the head girl of the group. She cried.'

biff
Although spina bifida is a very serious birth defect, resulting in severe

loss of motor function, it's got around five syllables in it. That's a lot of syllables for children with short attention spans to be remembering.

So sufferers of spina bifida became known as biffs, or biffers, which was *much* easier to remember. If lacking in humanity.

big bender in a bun A Wimpy burger. Perhaps the first time that children realised that advertising people did this sort of thing on purpose.

bigchiefweightumlegs A fat child. He doesn't have to be Native American; in fact it would probably be racist if he was.

big cock randy mountains Popular rewording of the assembly nonsense song 'Big Rock Candy Mountain'. As a bonus, the first verse contained the line 'a burly bum went hiking'.

binning The smallest child in the class was placed, arse-first, in the bin, so that his knees were forced into his armpits. His range of movement was thus reduced to a useless flail. The bin was then lifted on to the teacher's desk, as everyone took their normal positions in the class.

If you were lucky, the child would thrash in such panic that the bin would fall off the desk, leaving him stunned and semi-conscious in a pile of rubbish on the floor. This would seem more incriminating to the teacher, as it simply looked like the child went mental in the bin, and lost consciousness through maniacal hyperventilation.

bisto 1. A fart. As in, 'Aaaah … *Bisto.*' **2.** Also used as a synonym for 'fantastic' – combined with French to create the sophisticated compliment: *c'est la bisto*.

When used to complement a fart, the two uses combine to create the image of an adorable thick soupy brown fart. This phrase could be accompanied by kissing the thumb and forefinger in that unmistakably French way. And wearing onions around your neck. And riding your bicycle to a whorehouse.

bite-size sandwiches At dinner time, find a child with sandwiches wrapped in cling film. Bite through the cling film (without breaking it), to reduce the sandwiches to a pulp of well chewed but hygienic bite-sized chunks. On its most charitable interpretation, this is similar to your mum cutting up tricky pieces of meat for you.

Caution must be taken not to leave a full set of teeth marks, however, as there was a detective show where the murderer was once identified from teeth marks left on the body. So you must be careful just in case the teachers called the police.

b.j.d. Billy Joel Detention. A curious but effective punishment in which children were forced to watch the video to 'Uptown Girl'.

blimeys A pair of breasts so outstanding that you feel compelled to say 'blimey'.

bloo poo
1. Shit in sink.

2. Fill sink with bottles of Quink.
3. Send unimportant child to inform caretaker that someone's filled the sink with ink.
4. Assume casual-looking stance by urinals along with mates.
5. Attempt not to giggle.
6. Caretaker arrives, and attempts to unplug sink *WITHOUT GLOVES*. *Unnecessary shouting*.
7. Bloo poo!
8. Oh yeah, run.

blue goldfish A creature that resides just around the U-bend of the school toilet.

If you were asked whether you wanted to see a blue goldfish, and you replied yes, there would normally be someone kind enough to push your head into the toilet to help you see it. Sometimes a couple of flushes would be required to entice the blue goldfish out of its lair.

Although most attempts to find the blue goldfish ended in disappointment, at least you now knew where it was, and could teach other people.

bmw An expensive car, or a black man's willy, depending on whether you've touched one or not.

bmx BMX boys have a lot of fun, sticking their handlebars up their bum. It's true.

bogieflys These beautiful symmetrical creatures, half butterfly half bogey, are found in freshly used and reopened handkerchiefs. They come in colours ranging from yellow to green, and the rare and exquisite red variety.

bomb the argentinians A popular chant in the UK during the Falklands Conflict, the last war which everyone seemed to think was OK. The chant was accompanied by stamping of feet and banging on the walls, a clear sign of impatience that the Argentinians weren't being bombed enough.

boob ladies 'Imaginary kidnappers who kidnap children in order to show them their boobs. The Boob Lady game was a popular one. We played it a lot.'

boyfriends, you have many A method of divining exactly how many boyfriends your classmate has.

- Sneak up behind your victim, and count silently whilst covering your mouth with your hand.
- When the person notices, they must cover their own mouth to stop your counting.
- Once they have covered their mouth, shout '[Victim's name] has [whatever number you had managed to count to, or alternatively a completely made-up number] boyfriends!'

This game is restricted to pre-puberty, after which a more common insult is 'you have no boyfriend because you smell of period'.

break friends Opposite of 'make friends'. A remarkably civil ceremony signifying that all friendly interaction would cease. Performed with a sharp, single handshake. You could, at any time, 'make friends' again, for instance if you want to borrow a ruler, with this rhyme: 'Make friends, make friends, never never break friends. If you do, you'll catch the 'flu, and that will be the end of you.'

Warning: This is childish.

brian may A song to the tune of 'Knick Knack Paddywhack' that can mortally insult someone whose name has two syllables. In this example, we will use Richard.

> Richard's gay, Richard's gay,
> Richard's name is Brian May.

Works equally well with Darren Day.

See also: gay

brillo pads 1. Pointless re-extension of 'brill' to make it just as long as the originally abbreviated word, 'brilliant'. A bit posh. You probably deserve to get hit if you use this. **2.** A hairstyle on white people which is more naturally at home on black people. Sporters of the Brillo Pad can either spend all their money on hair gel, or bide their time and wait for the comparative tolerance of sixth form college.

brilly burgers Exclamation of camp delight. If you are a teacher, this is a rather ill-advised outburst to make to a group of teenagers in a state of homosexual panic.

bronno A female poor person who lives in a caravan and wears the same clothes every day. Possibly derived from *Neighbours*' Bronwyn, who was actually very nice-looking. Also possibly derived from the colour brown, which is the colour that poo is.

bruce wee The punchline of one of many jokes based on the name Bruce Lee.

'What kicks you in the face and holds your golf balls? – Bruce Tee.'

'What punches you in the stomach then walks away? – Bruce Me.' (Follow this joke by punching your friend in the stomach then walking away.)

'Who mastered the one-inch-punch and is traditionally served with fish and chips, can also be served mushy, and grows in pods? – Bruce Pea.'

Also consider Scooby Poo, Wee-Man

and the Masters of the Pooniverse, and the Abba song, Knowing Wee, Knowing Poo.

brucie bonus An unexpected continuation of a bullying session. Simply finish your primary attack, make a reassuring gesture such as a pat on the back to let the victim know their torture is over, then scream *'Brucie Bonus!'* and do the same thing again.

b.t. 1. Someone who has been circumcised. Effective, because people generally wonder what the hell the person's getting at. The punchline 'I've been cut off' should be delivered in the howl of someone undergoing an unanaesthetised circumcision. **2.** A more modern variant, *Big Tits*. Requires two participants, and a big-titted girl. One boy shouts 'beeee... teeee...', the other runs up to punch the tits and shouts 'Cellnet!' Then both boys run away, because everyone knows punching girls in the tits gives them cancer.
See also: stinger

b.t. baracus A child who was too poor to have a landline in their house, and was forced to use payphones. It could be added that the phone box was actually their home, and that attempts on *Record Breakers* to fit as many people into a phone box as possible was actually their family coming around for Christmas.

This currently works for children without mobile phones.

buck-a-chow An expression of delight or surprise based on a 1970s funky wah-wah guitar, of the sort that would accompany Dirty Harry in a rooftop chase of bad guys.

bugger me As the true meaning of the word 'bugger' became known, the phrase 'bugger me' (also 'fuck me') became somewhat dangerous. The responses vary depending on the sophistication of your company.
Revolted: 'Eur, you fucking queer.'
Regular: 'Eur, no thanks.'
Double Bluff: 'I'll wait until after PE, when you've loosened up.'

Camp Camaraderie: 'Ooh, duckie pops!'

bulls' eyes

'In biology, we were given bulls' eyes to dissect. Obviously this was an important lesson for anyone who was looking for a career in bovine ophthalmology. For the rest of us, we were happy to discover that the stuff at the back (presumably optic nerves and shit) was very sticky. This meant that by the time the teacher got back from break, there were 20 bulls' eyes stuck to the blackboard glaring down at her.

'To give Miss credit, she pretended to be as startled as she must have been the first time a class did this, ten years ago.'

bullying
See: other entries

bum chums

Two boys attaining any level of close friendship. Walking together, talking together, indulging in any manly displays of affection, all this was just foreplay. They were *bum chums*, and even if they didn't actually bum each other, then they touched each other's bums somehow. They *must have*.

bumdrag

The act of grabbing the victim's ankles, and dragging him across the school playground. If you drag using the trouser legs alone, you can pull the pants down enough to cause *bumdrag* on actual bumcheeks.

bummer

Whether someone was a bummer or not could easily be divined from the pitch and timbre of their farts. A tight, peachy squit meant you were OK, whereas a resonant, guttural blotch implied that your extra-curricular bumming activities had permanently loosened your sphincter, which resembled a tattered windsock.

bumming

1. To borrow. 'Bum us some money, Laura says she'll let me touch her tits for 50p.' **2.** Quick, efficient way to mildly embarrass. Any movement of the victim is interpreted as bumming, and the item closest to them is the thing being bummed. Anything can potentially be bummed: tables, bags, even air. 'Bumming air' can be used as a general term for 'moving'. **3.** Surprisingly acceptable act of simulated buggery. See *man train*. **4.** When sharing a cigarette, to suck so firmly and indelicately to leave the butt wet and/or covered in lip balm. Doing this *bums* the cigarette. You have *bummed* it. Regular cigarette *bumming* will stop people wanting to share a crafty B&H with you whenever there's *seven minutes* spare.

bumming bushes, the

'As everyone knows, Gayness – like vampirism – is spread through intimate contact. Therefore, if you approached *The Bumming Bushes* at the far end of the playing field, you were asking for it. Hidden in these bushes was anywhere between one and five naked men who would bum any boy who came too close. They would drag him into the bushes and bum him until he liked it. They would then release him into the world, to spread his condition.

'A brave group of boys once stormed the bushes, and found no naked men; but they *did* find a few lolly sticks, an empty can and some string. This was all the evidence needed to confirm that some victim had been tied up and bummed with such vigour that a refreshment break had been necessary.

'As the legend grew bolder, the naked men were given names. There was Ram Bottom – the leader, Captain Kinky, Big Billy Bendy Bollocks and two others.'

bundy

The favourite half-bullying attack of Arnold Hill Comprehensive, derived from either the then-WWF wrestling star King Kong Bundy, or the serial killer Ted Bundy. Accompanied by the battle cry of 'Ooww, Bundy …', the elbow was raised above the head and brought down on the victim, as the assailant launched himself wholesale into the attack.

A real crowd-pleaser, and not actually that painful. It isn't a bundy if the attacker's feet don't leave the ground during the blow. They may cry 'Bundy', but they are wrong.

bundys bank A place in Germany where all the unperformed *bundies* are kept, waiting patiently to be delivered.

burpees A combination of a squat thrust and a star jump that contains the word burp, which is a funny word because burping is funny.

burp 'n' blow The act of burping into your cupped hands and releasing the finger seal with a simultaneous blow of the stench in the direction of your mate, or victim. *See illustrations overleaf.*

burp tennis A two-player game, in which the players would face each other about 20 feet apart. The game would start with the first player to swing his imaginary racket. He would then emit a loud burp when the racket made contact with the imaginary ball.

The game was won in two ways: either one player would hit an Ace (a burp so loud that it would bring him close to vomiting, much to the applause of the audience), or a player would just run out of burps.
See also: farting league

bus tipping When the double-decker bus made a sharp left, all boys on the top deck hurled themselves violently towards the right-hand side of the bus, in order to tip it over. Afterwards everyone agreed that they definitely got the wheels off the road that time.

burp 'n' blow

Put your lips to the loading bay
and deposit your gusty cargo.

An optional 'targeting' stage,
using your little fingers as
a crosshair until you settle
on your victim.

Before too long (you are
constantly losing heat and
stench density), release your
burp and blow it in the face
of your victim.

C c

cak A game in which you cak yourself. A cricket ball was thrown towards the top of a horse-chestnut tree. All participants then stood under the branches, as nature's Pachinko decided who might receive a skull-splitting thunk to the head.

Horse-chestnut trees were preferred as they are particularly noisy, and in season a secondary rain of conkers added to the excitement. When in full leaf it was also difficult to see through the branches, so the mystery was complete.

By looking up, you were risking a broken nose – if you were especially unfortunate, then you might get that thing you heard about, where your nose goes into your brain, and kills you.

'*The last thing he smelled was his own brain,*' the coroner would tut sadly to himself.

camel club A pre-sexual organisation. A former member explains:

'To become a member of the club you had to be '*humped*' by the head Camel himself, or any other member of the club. Some standing was gained from being humped by the original Camel, though – it was like the extra kudos you get by being told off by the headmaster. Humping involved a bumping of the chest on to the humpee's back, accompanied by a cry of '*HUMP!*' Note — no genital contact was required.

'Everyone wanted to be humped, although no one really knew why they wanted to, or why it felt so right and so wrong. All we knew is that once we'd been humped, we had to hump someone else.

'The Camel Club developed in odder directions when the lead Camel pointed out on a map where Camel Land was — presumably he would lead us there one day — and issued coded orders that no one understood.

'The lead Camel left our school (in a kind of Ascension) after his club disbanded, due to a lack of any non-members to hump.'

camel fart
On a canteen menu board, possibly the most amusing amendment of Caramel Tart.

captain sadness
A rank of sadness attained by those who have ever said, 'Actually, I'm a *dark* elf,' as though dark elves were somehow less pathetic than their paler brethren. Higher ranks of sadness can be attained by concurrently being good at chess or having a basin haircut.

cash club
Partial homage to *Fight Club.*

1. Ten to twenty boys stand in a circle.
2. The members of the circle throw whatever small change or trinkets they can muster into the centre of the ring. The amount of money (or cool stuff) slowly piles up.
3. At some point, someone will decide that the reward offsets the risk, and try to grab the money.
4. Everyone jumps on that person whilst trying to get the cool stuff for themselves.

For the next 30 seconds, the situation degenerates into a writhing, screaming free-for-all, a mosh pit without the music or the kindness. If you are quick, you could make a profit of 10 to 20p, and only get your hand crushed a couple of times.

This is particularly revolting when you have rich and poor kids playing the same game, and the rich kids simply watch the poor ones fight over such a trifling pittance, and laugh with their hands on their hips, and boast about how many geese they're eating for dinner.

catch 22 The Catch 22; a staple of the bully since before the phrase Catch 22 existed. The following may not be Catch 22s in the strictest sense, but try pointing that out to a bully. It won't get you any fewer beatings. Playground Catch 22s are essentially situations where you will find it very hard not to look stupid or get punched.

- **Did you watch *Spackers Say No* last night?** You didn't. So you say no. You spacker. Escape from this by saying 'I missed it' or 'I missed it, but I did see *Wankers Say "Did You Watch Spackers Say No Last Night"'*

- **Have you got AIDS?** When you say no, they reply, '*Are you positive?*', leaving you forced to acknowledge that although you haven't gone full-blown, it's only a matter of time. Escape by replying, 'I'm absolutely sure.'

- **If your dad and a whore were drowning in a lake and you had to choose, who would you save?** Only a child with deranged priorities would leave his father to drown, so when you reply 'my father', they will say, 'What, and leave your mum to drown?'

- **Are you a homo?** Perhaps the first Catch 22. Reply yes, and you are a homosexual. Reply no, and you're not a homo sapien. Not terribly insulting or funny, but an all-time classic.

- **Are you ace?** More tenuously, reply yes to this question and you will hear 'Ha ha, ace is card, card is paper, paper is thick and so are you'. This rhyme deftly ignores the fact that paper is in no way thick. Escape with 'Ace? I'm brilliant!' or 'Paper isn't thick'.

Finally, the gay trilogy:

- **If a gay jumped on your back ... would you let him stay or pull him off?**

- **If you were on a bus full of gays, would you get off?**
- **Do your parents know you're gay?**

catshagging Everyone knows someone who has supposedly shagged a cat. One day, they will reopen the cases of all those who have been unfairly condemned; until then, simply know that you were not alone.
See also: extreme catshagging

ceiling dribbler Fill a little syringe from the science labs with fleg. Then slam the syringe down on the table as hard as you can, plunger first. This will cause the loogies to rocket up and stick to the ceiling. It will then slowly drip down for the next hour, in long gloopy strands. Best done over someone else's desk.

chain reaction Walk around the painted lines of the netball court, football pitch, etc. You are not allowed to change directions. If you bump into someone else, you have to sing the chorus of Diana Ross's hit single, 'Chain Reaction'.

chalky balls 1. The victim is held down by two assailants, while a third uses a piece of chalk to draw a set of male genitalia on the victim's black school trousers, in a crude oversized parody of the boy's real genitalia. The victim now has three choices. One, spend the next 20 minutes openly rubbing his crotch to remove the artwork. Two, run to the toilets to wash it off, making him look like he's pissed himself. Three, leave the offending artwork for all to see. Playground *Catch 22*-ing at its finest. **2.** If a teacher has the habit of resting his testicles on the corner of a table as he addresses the class, simply put chalk on the rim of the table. Use a whole packet of coloured chalk for *Technicolor Dreamtrousers*.

charity week Response to a request for usury services. *'Can you lend me 50p?'* could be answered with *'What do you think it is, Charity Week?'* Typically, denser characters took the insult to illogical conclusions, by giving this response to questions such as *'What time is it?'* (the correct answer to which is, of course, '*Time you got a watch*'). ***See also: go buy one***

cherry lips where the antelope roam

An insult for creamy-skinned boys or girls with rosy patches on their faces. A superior insult to 'Ding Dong, Avon Calling', as it completely robs the victim of any comeback. This is because, possibly, the image of antelope roaming freely from one lip to the other makes absolutely no sense.

chicken bumswing

A martial art invented and practised in secondary school. Opponents (one-on-one or team event) run at each other at high speed, jumping into the air, whilst turning so that the bums of each opponent clash. The main idea is to knock your opponent off balance in mid-air so that they land flat on the concrete and split their head open. It is also customary to chant 'chicken bumswing' in a mild quasi-Oriental voice whilst in battle.
See also: head open, he's split his

chicken group

'Some remedial classes, because of the innately gentle nature of the mentally unexcellent, are sometimes charged with the care of several chickens. At Great Sankey High School, the *chicken group* lasted until a leading member took it upon himself to destroy all the chickens with a spade.'

chin, uses of the

- **ayatollah, ayatollah!**: To signify the winning of an argument. Once you have *sussed* your opponent, you may run around combing your imaginary ayatollah's beard. Should a friend be at hand, they may grab at your chin, then run off, extending your invisible beard to unimaginable lengths before somebody cuts it off.
- **chin nuggets**: Simple assault. Seize your victim in the classic 'nuggy' position, with their head clamped underneath your arm. Then rub your chin all over their head, allowing yourself to dribble freely. Whilst doing this, make gleeful gurgling noises. This special attack is good for humiliation only, as it doesn't really hurt.

- **chinny beef**: Once a victim has been taunted to the point where they start lashing out, sulking or (at best) crying, it is then that the aggressor may move in, and say *'chinny beef'*. This is usually accompanied with a raking of his chin with the fingers of one hand and a simultaneous action on the victim's chin with the other. No taunting is complete until the victim has a *'chinny on'*.

- **chinny reckon, chin wag**: When a colleague makes a wildly wrong statement, such as 'I saw *Jaws 5* when I was on holiday in America', then the *chinny reckon* informs them that they are wrong.

- **chin violin**: As above but accompanied by an improvised hoe-down addressing the nature of lying, much like Josie Lawrence might have done on *Whose Line Is It Anyway?*, whilst playing your chin with an imaginary bow.

- **jimmy hill, tutankhamun, etcetera**: Evolved forms of the chinny reckon. Whereas chinny reckon involves scratching your chin, these remixes can involve scratching thin air where your chin would be, if it was the size of Jimmy Hill's. Even better, Tutankhamun's death mask. *See illustrations overleaf.*

- **chinny barbados**: As above, but accompanied with the tongue in the lower lip and wild grunting.

chinese rude finger

Giving someone the finger, except you stick up your pinky rather than your middle finger. Then you must bellow in a crap Chinese accent, *'Chinese rude finger!'* This avoids the ire of the teachers as the gesture is neither rude nor particularly Chinese. ***See also: fake swearing***

chinese whispers

An easily sabotaged game. All it takes is for one child to say, 'Mr Gardner smells of piss,' and you're away. Teachers will not know who to punish, the children will sense the shift of power and the teacher will be a skeleton left to bake in the sun before the final bell.

Teachers: Avoid this situation arising by making each child write down what they actually said.

On a related note, *Chinese Whispers* is crap if, when you are not sure of a word, you replace it with 'something' instead of a word it sounded like. You're supposed to say what it sounded like, you see. If defeats the object of the game to have the last person saying 'something' 15 times. You *idiots*.

ching chong chinaman

A touching ode to an incompetent Oriental farmer:

> *Ching Chong Chinaman*
> *went to milk a cow;*
> *Ching Chong Chinaman*
> *didn't know how.*
> *Ching Chong Chinaman*
> *pulled the wrong tit;*
> *Ching Chong Chinaman*
> *covered in shit.*

In retrospect it's hard to imagine what 'the wrong tit' could possibly mean, although I suppose it could be the cow's tail. Sensing his career in farming was not to be, our poor stereotype moved into retail management.

> *Ching Chong Chinaman*
> *bought a little shop,*
> *and all he sold was peppermint rock.*
> *He pissed in a bottle*
> *and he called it pop,*
> *Ching Chong Chinaman*
> *bought a little shop.*

It is hoping against hope that this venture was any more successful than the last.

choose wisely
Based on the grail selection scene at the end of *Indiana Jones and the Last Crusade*.

Present the victim with two closed palms. Tell them to '*choose wisely*'. Whichever choice is made precipitates a violent assault, followed by gravely intoning 'he chose poorly' in the voice of a 700-year-old knight.

chubbing
The spraying of Deep Heat on to the testicles. Like all classic forms of torture, both immensely painful and largely non-fatal.

chug
To masturbate. As a noun, you are a '*chugger*', and if you are a prolific wanker, you are a '*chuggernaut*'.

chin stroking

A simple chin stroke. This will suffice for regular lies, such as 'sorry I'm late, I had an allergic reaction to something, but am better now'.

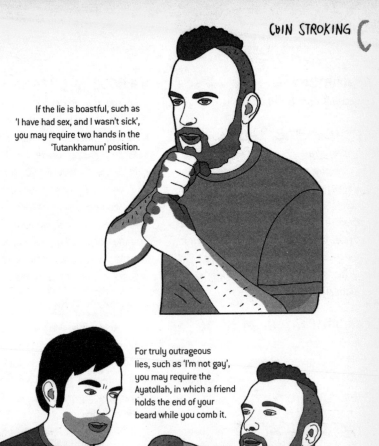

If the lie is boastful, such as 'I have had sex, and I wasn't sick', you may require two hands in the 'Tutankhamun' position.

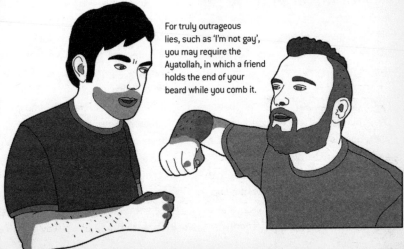

For truly outrageous lies, such as 'I'm not gay', you may require the Ayatollah, in which a friend holds the end of your beard while you comb it.

chummer
Advanced *bummer*, or, if you will, *bum chum* third dan.

circle game, the
A fairly well-known game.

The object of the circle game is to get your opponent to see the 'circle', which is formed from your forefinger and thumb. If you get them to look at the circle, then you get to punch them in the arm.

To see an advanced circling technique, turn to page 46.

circumcision, what is?
A futile question designed to test the infinite patience of religious education teachers. The class to get the most explanations wins.

clacker knackers
The name for a boy who, having undergone an operation to his testicles, is lunatic enough to share his experience with his best friend – believing perhaps that his friend won't sell him down the river for the 10 seconds of attention that a cool bollock-related story will get him.

clarence boddicker
A villain from the film *Robocop*, and the first quotable hero for many children. If you have ever pushed someone over and said '*Can you fly, Bobby?*' or if you've said '*Bitches – leave!*' to your modern-day wife's friends, then you have Clarence Boddicker to thank.

Another classic *Robocop* quote – '*I'd buy that for a dollar*'. To be used near a woman with exceptionally large breasts, preferably someone's mum.

classical wank
Classic urban fable, told with very little variation, although in this version the boy is listening to *Beethoven's Fifth*. Basically, this:

- Boy decides to have sophisticated wank, using headphones and closing his eyes.
- To *Beethoven's Fifth*, the boy masturbates to stringy completion.
- Upon opening his eyes, a steaming cup of tea is next to his bed.

So, the boy deduces that Mother has watched him wank, and can never leave his room again. You can almost imagine the mother tip-toeing to the bedside table, silently putting the cup down, and running downstairs to tell the father how much she's just messed with their son's mind.

Well, you could if it wasn't a lie, anyway.

cling film
Not a proper or acceptable substitute for a contraceptive, or a lunchbox.

clint eastwood fan club
Inform a child how great Clint Eastwood is, and how much he or she loves them. Then make a special Clint Eastwood cap for the child to wear in lessons. This is a rather shonky origami affair with the word Clint written across it in capital letters. *See illustration overleaf.*
See also: pen fifteen club

coke-can turd
At some point in all children's lives, they will be called upon to witness a gigantic turd resting in a toilet bowl. The awe that is accorded to this turd often leads to boasting competitions, in which ever more audacious claims are made.

The Coke-can turd is the most disturbingly oversized yet unnervingly believable girth. ***See also: bumming***

cool
If someone uncool claims to be cool, then it stands for *crazy on old ladies*.

cool gang, the
'What a school-mate was said to have joined when he discarded his GameBoy, signed up for driving lessons and started sneaking off to the pub at night with other cool-gang members instead of meeting the rest of us near the spooky old house around lunchtime on Saturday. Used with a jealous sneer.'

cow tipping
Rural fun based on the cow's inability to move sideways. Tippers take a run up at the sleeping or docile cow and try to push it over. If successful, this often results in the cow being killed. This practice genuinely does happen – a possibly mythical extension was that the tipper would take a run up, hit the cow, slip through the cow's legs and get landed on by a freshly tipped cow. Then they *both* die. *Brucie Bonus!*

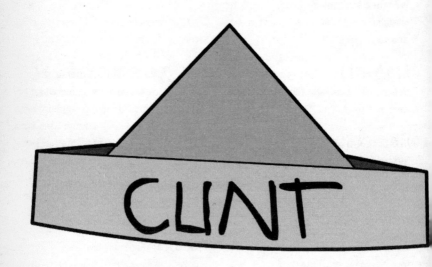

The hat that signifies that the wearer, at any
given time, is the number one fan of Clint Eastwood.

Crog, Croggy Also known as a *backey*, or *takey*. Hitching a ride on a bike clearly designed with only one rider in mind. The compromised lateral stability of the bike, and the fact that the 'passenger' has to stick his legs out, invokes terror in pedestrians, road users and both riders as the lurching four-legged monster blunders between kerb and road.

A boy was rumoured to have slid off the seat and on to the wheel, and had his scrotum 'eaten' by the mudguard. Once enough people heard this rumour it was accepted as truth.

Also, the 'barrey', in which the passenger sits on the handlebars, entirely obscuring the view of the rider. And crushing his (own) nuts.

Cuffer One who wipes their nose/arse/mouth/whatever on their cuffs to such an extent there is a build-up of crap pretty much to the elbow. Just a tramp, basically.

Cuntstack A sophisticated insult based on a misunderstanding.

'Walking cautiously home from school behind some big fat year nines, I overheard one say to the other, "You're a cuntstack!" I gaped, wide-eyed, thinking I had stumbled across an ingenious new insult. I later found out the bloke was called Kevin Stack, and his mate was therefore merely calling him a cunt, but this didn't stop me using "cuntstack" at every possible opportunity.'

D d

daddy A cranefly, after the routine removal of all six of its long legs.

dangly-greeny Also known as *abseilors*. Heavily greened fleg that are dangled from the mouth over the face of the victim, who is either being held down or kneeled on. The trick is to add enough mucus to allow the sucking back up of the greeny, making this a sophisticated form of mental cruelty rather than physical abuse. If you ignore the fact you are kneeling on your victim's chest.

dead actually, my mum is The proper response to 'Does your mother let you do that at home?'

dead brother A game you play with a younger sibling or friend. The rules are simple. Simply pretend that the younger person is dead. If they talk to you, ignore them and comment on how tragic their loss was; they were so young and showed such promise! If they start screaming, comment that it's almost like they're here, in the room with you. You can *almost* hear their voice.

The victim of this game will eventually panic, and require an adult to prove that they are still alive.

ded embryo One of the many band names carrying on the spirit of teenage punk. Other names gathered from around the country are *Hevi Sosij*, *Lesbian Ashtray*, *Bigfoot and the Groincrushers*, *Uncle Fester* (whose local hit 'Bush Dog' remains a high tribute to sociology teacher Mrs Bush).

Dad's Big Log were forced to change their name, although they managed to keep the initials with *Dark Brown Lada*. *ZX Rectum* may have raised a smile or two, but it was widely acknowledged that *The Myra Hindley Creche Facility* had gone one step too far when their posters went up around the school.

The basic principles of starting a teenage band are simple:
1. Choose band name.
2. Choose first album title.
3. Design first album cover.
4. Plan how to spend first million made by album.
5. Disband for artistic reasons.

der-brain Any child whose brain is full of der is a der-brain. Der, when located in the brain, makes you do stupid things. The more der there is in your brain, the longer the word der becomes. For instance, if you have pulled a push door, a simple 'der' will suffice. If you have just bitten your fingers whilst putting a crisp into your mouth, a more protracted 'deeeeer' may be required.

diarrhoea If you're walking down the street, and you feel something on your feet, chances are it's diarrhoea. Similarly, if you're walking past the docks, and you feel it in your socks, this too might be diarrhoea. And if you eat too many beans, you run the very real risk of feeling it in your jeans. Diarrhoea. Diarrhoea.

Interestingly enough, 'Air Raid' read backwards is diarrhoea.

dickhead The act of rubbing your cheeks at someone, then gobbing in their face. For added authenticity, immediately fart on their leg then fall asleep. Tch! *Men*!

dick on tongue A dick is drawn on a Rizla, then placed upon the tongue. The saliva quickly sends the Rizla transparent, leaving the very realistic impression of a dick tattoo on the tongue. When people see this, they should shout, 'Dick On Tongue!'

dicksplash One of the insults that, in use, makes the user more of one than the person they say it to. Also in this range are *plonker* and *tosspot*.
See also: egg dribble; sly old fox; emery dermis

dictation By quietly repeating the words of the teacher a moment after they say them, as though you are concentrating very hard, it is possible to get the person next to you to start copying down what *you* are saying.

Once you have his attention, stop talking about the properties of oxygen and start talking about a blue monkey with a gigantic penis.

ding dong dairylea An obscure term for 'smelly cock', derived via the popular 'cheesy bellender'.

ding dong ding dong
> Ding dong ding dong,
> your nose is that long.

Sung to the tune of Big Ben striking. Childish.

dirty duck After successfully getting someone to turn around when you say, 'Look over there – it's Bobby Davro!', compound their shame by taunting them with the following rhyme:
> *Made you look,*
> *Dirty duck,*
> *You stuck your head in cow muck.*

You see? They stuck their head in cow muck. Because they turned around. Also consider, '*Made you look, made you stare, made you lose your underwear.*'

distance pissing
- *Horizontal Distance Pissing* – contestants stand at the trough, urinating normally. Then walk backwards, striving to maintain a constant stream of piss into the trough. Returning to the trough before the stream turns into a trickle is considered a graceful flourish. The first

casualty in this game is the floor.

- *Vertical Distance Pissing* – contestants stand at a fixed distance from a wall, and piss up it. The person to reach the highest point on the wall wins. Contestants may play together, or take it in turns to beat the previous best wet patch.

It is quite possible to piss in your own face, or to suffer *Lucozade* during the vertical distance pissing game. Hitting the ceiling is possible only by the advanced technique of helmet pinching. **See also: lucozade**

do you use toilet paper?

The soothsayer would take the victim's palm, and attempt to tell his future. He would ask:

'*Do you live in this town?*'
'*Do you live in a house?*'
'*Does it have a kitchen?*'
'*Does it have some stairs?*'
'*Does it have a bathroom?*'
'*Does it have a toilet?*'
'*Do you use toilet paper?*'

The victim answered 'yes' to all these questions. They were asked slowly, to create an involving and eerie atmosphere, and all the time, a nauseatingly intimate contact was maintained with their palm. After the last question, the soothsayer would say 'I don't, I use my hands.'

If you were the victim, and aware of the procedure, you could effect a daring reversal by answering the last question with, 'No, I use *my* hands.'

A variant – 'Do you use your left or your right hand to wipe your arse?' Whatever the answer, reply, 'Eur, I use toilet paper.'

domball

Not to be confused with *DoomBall*. Similar to Australian rules football, two (sloppily defined) teams of people would attempt to score by carrying, kicking or throwing a Dominic to their end of the common room. Additional points were allegedly available for mid-play manoeuvres such as *posting*. Games were started unpredictably with the rallying cry of 'DOMBALL!' whenever a Dominic was in the common room, which became decreasingly frequent as the game grew in popularity. **See also: posting**

don't cross the streams

After seeing *Ghostbusters*, children became aware of the danger, when using nuclear laser weaponry, of 'crossing the streams'. As the closest that most children had to nuclear laser weaponry was their penis, this translated into a game where two children would piss into the same bowl whilst howling in fear. Should the streams have crossed, the children would have undergone total particle reversal, which would have involved getting a lot of piss on the walls.

For 10 years before *Ghostbusters*, this game was known as 'Lightsabres', and both parties would just wave their willies around and go 'fvwm, fvwm', like real Jedi.

For the 1977 years before *that*, the game was known as Jesus's Cross, and should the streams cross, you had to shout 'Jesus's Cross!', so everyone would know what had happened.

don't crowd me, fans

Said by the wanker in the middle of a crowd of people waiting to get through a door. Could be followed by, 'I'll sign autographs later.'

don't cry, dry your eyes

An odd paradox; the more people singing this to a fellow pupil who is crying, the more they cry. Absolutely baffling.

don't go near him, he's psycho

A self-fulfilling prophecy, when repeated often enough. The victim will become so starved of human interaction that they will, eventually, become psycho.

don't touch what you can't afford

Get off my bag. Get off my coat. Stop touching me. This actually worked more charmingly when a poor kid said '*don't touch what you can't afford*' when someone brushed up against their snot-covered Parka, prompting cries of '*as if*' and '*oo-eeeeer*'.

door corner crush

When fully opened back upon itself, some classroom doors create a kind of tiny triangular cell, made from two corner walls and a door. An unpopular pupil may be safely contained in this cell. Then, every single school bag within reach may be hurled over the top, lightly crushing the victim.

double agents A despicable breed that shares interests and sympathy with the geeks, but has somehow managed to end up with a popular set of friends. These *double agents* may even go to their geek friends' houses at the weekend to paint little lead goblins, but within school hours they are inexplicably distant, their one concession to the sham of a friendship being the fact that they only laugh half-heartedly at the routine destruction of the geeks' belongings.

d.s. *Directed Study*. A cosy euphemism; *directed study* consisted of nothing more than removing a disruptive pupil from the classroom and forcing them to study in isolation. Because entire classrooms are rarely free for this purpose, the troublemaker will generally be ushered into a store room with some crayons, paper and a half-meant order not to drink the cleaning fluid.

This is the method by which most maladjusted cartoonists have been created.

duck! A potentially brain-damaging game played – in general – with the class Warhammer fan. It involved shouting '*duck!*', and then hitting the victim around the head with, well, anything.

After some time, the subject would get wise to the game, and take steps to defend himself. At this point, the rules were amended to allow shouting '*duck!*' **after** hitting him with, well, anything.

duffel coat tents Constructed, like coats made from animal skins, by the zipping together of five or so duffel coats. Then, climb inside and giggle until bored. Ski coats, which have detachable arms (in case you become trapped under a tree whilst skiing, and need to sacrifice a limb), could be made into a ski ensemble, by unzipping the arms, then zipping the arms to each other and wearing them as trousers. Then you could swan around like the lord of the manor, even if you do walk like a lunatic wearing a loaded nappy.

durex club Sung to the tune of the Country Life butter advert, it goes something like this:

> Oh, we are the lads
> from the Durex Club,
> And you'll never get a better bit
> of rubber on your knob;
> It sticks to your dick like evo-stick,
> And you can't get it off in the morning

In later life, you may find it better etiquette to remove the condom immediately after sex. Partners may be unhappy with the idea of you leaving it on until the morning.

dusting 1. Patting a friend on the back with a concealed board rubber. The resulting chalk stripe is nigh on irremovable, and the dust cloud evokes scenes from *Saving Private Ryan*. **2.** Making sure the board rubber is fully loaded, run up to someone and start battering the board rubber with your hand; or, better still, a second fully loaded board rubber. Skill (not the kind in the African medical dictionary) was required not to suffer blowback.

If blowback does occur, however, take advantage of the situation and have a cartoon fight, in which spectators will only see the occasional arm or leg coming out of the dust cloud as you shout 'Ooyah!' and 'Take that!'

dying spaceship Stack the entire class's chairs around the captain of the dying spaceship, then kick them over so that the captain is lost in a tangle of awkward metal and plastic. Just like in a real dying spaceship scenario, the captain can be hurt very badly.

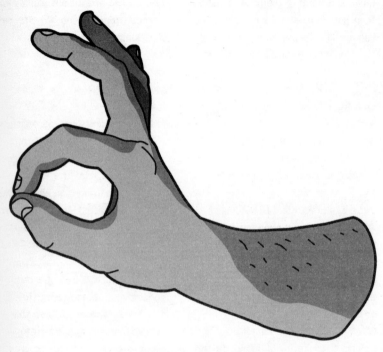

See: Circle Game. If you are holding this book
under waist height, then please ask someone
nearby to punch you in the arm.

Ee

eagle, stare it out like an Advice given to pupils complaining about sun in their eyes, by a less sympathetic English teacher. Half-plausible until you realise that 1) eagles don't stare at the sun and 2) you'd go blind.

ee by gum A questionnaire devised to find trends in belly, bum and ball flexibility in the under 10s:

> Ee by gum, can your belly
> touch your bum?
> Can your balls hang low?
> Can you tie them in a bow?
> Can you slap them on the ceiling
> when you get a funny feeling?

eenie meenie minie mo A generations-old rhyme that was forced to change in an age of political correctness.

> Eenie meenie minie mo,
> catch a nigger by the toe.
> If he squeals, let him go,
> Eenie meenie minie mo.

Nigger was changed to tiger as soon as someone realised that the practice of hunting black people and only letting them go if they squealed might be seen as inconsistent with multiculturalism. So, nigger was changed to tiger, and squeal was changed to growl, and racism was eradicated at a stroke.

egg dribble An insult that makes no sense, and has only been used once. It was stammered by a child so angry that he simply said two words that sounded vaguely like they belonged in an insult somewhere.

The response? *'I'm a what? Did you call me an egg dribble? What's that? Is it nice?'*

See also: sly old fox; emery dermis

eggie eggie sa sa 'A mysteriously oppressive practice invented by a group of boys on a school trip. The girls would sit on a table in the boys' room, and the boys would circle round the table rubbing a set of imaginary breasts. Whilst doing this, they would chant, *'Eggie Eggie Sa Sa'*. After some time, the simple monotony and semi-sexuality of this process would scare the girls, who would run around screaming.

'Teachers rarely interrupted this process, perhaps scared to dabble in that which they didn't understand.'

egging Make a fist on someone's head, tap it down with your other hand, and slowly drag both hands down the scalp. This experience is exactly the same as having an egg gently tapped on your head, as those of us from loving egg-tapping families will know. *See illustration overleaf.*

eggy banner As in, *'Who just waved an eggy banner?'* A fart.

eggydemic A particularly obnoxious fart that moves throughout the room, causing despair and wailing, and much beating of chests.

elastic divide
1. Recruit a friend.
2. Find a smaller child who has his gloves attached to his coat on elastic.
3. Each grab a glove, and pull as far as the science of elastic allows.
4. Run around for a bit, then let go.

electric beard, the A test of endurance. You will need around 15-20 paper clips and a 12-volt power source (the 9v portable version has a very limited battery life). Next string the paper clips together and attach them like a beard – over your chin with the ends of the chain coming down behind your ears. Now attach the power source. The winner, naturally, is the one who can withstand the agony for longest, although after the first person people will probably say, 'Nah, you win, mate.'

elmo The fat bloke out of *Brush Strokes*, therefore any fat person in any class in any school, from 1986-88. The fat bloke was also in *Chelmsford 123*, with a similarly stupid, fat-sounding name. This caught on for a brief while but, appalling as *Brush Strokes* was, it was better than *Chelmsford 123*.

In later years, during the 80s' rise of the Yuppie, the character Elmo hilariously opened his own wine bar, 'Elmo Putney's Wine Bar'. Thus, any place where more than one fat person congregated became known as Elmo Putney's Wine Bar. Which, to be fair, sounded much classier than 'the queue for the ice cream van' or 'the spot outside the nurses' office where you pick up inhalers'. **See also: goof troop**

e.l.p. Ever Lasting Protection, against the lurgy, cooties, fleas, etcetera. Administered with an invisible can of flea spray over the affected area of the body. Must be accompanied by a 'Tssss!' hissing sound – otherwise your pressurised can obviously isn't working, and no protection will be afforded. Alternately, mime a pump action sound and go, 'Ffft! Fffft! Ffft!'

Can also be used on chairs and desks that are suspected of having been sat at by anyone incontinent, smelly or unpopular. Ever Lasting Protection lasts for one hour.

emery dermis 'A deeply regrettable insult on the part of the inventor. Referring to the eczema of his opponent, and the emery board-like complexion of his epidermis, the insult just sort of hung there for a few seconds before the cries of "emery what?" and "say that again, you fucking ponce" let him know that he had lost the argument.'

egging

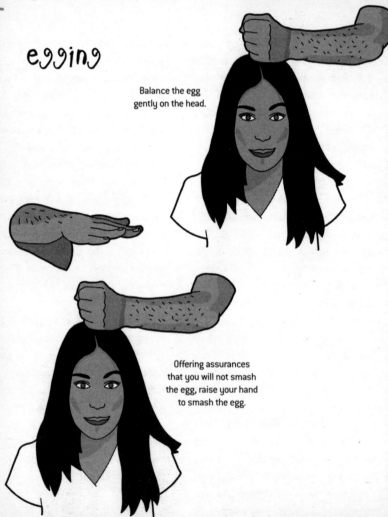

Balance the egg gently on the head.

Offering assurances that you will not smash the egg, raise your hand to smash the egg.

With a brisk
downward tap,
smash the egg.

At this stage, you realise
that this would be much
more fun with a real egg.

encrocklement Leathering of the anus, due to excess buggery. Not the proper medical name for it, which would probably be encrockleitis, or something.

eppie Abbreviation of epileptic fit. Usage: 'Jesus, don't have an eppie – it's just a bit of blood and some visible bone.' A common variation is the *schoolbag-swinging-eppie-fit*, where no one can get near, and the *eppie fitter* is crying snot.

This is a sign that you have pushed someone just far enough.

errhhhuuuuu! The sound you make after you ask someone what you get if you multiply one by one, and they answer 'two'.

error When something was typed into the BBC Computer that wasn't a BASIC command or a number, it would respond with the word 'ERROR'.
> chris is great and everyone likes him
ERROR
You can't argue with computers.

every gay boy deserves fudge In music lessons, a mnemonic that would help you remember the notes of the treble clef (E, G, B, D, F). Alternatively, Every Girl's Breasts Deserve Fondling. Or Fucking, if you're in the mood.

everything-proof shield-piercing bullets Another logical conclusion, alongside *infinity plus one*.
'Bang, bang. You're dead.'
'No, I've got a bulletproof shield.'
'But I shot you with nukerler missiles.'
'It's a nuclear-proof shield too.'
'OK, zap, zap. You're dead.'
'It's got laser-proof too. It's an every-thing-proof shield.'
'OK. I just got my everything-proof shield-piercing bullets and shot you. You're dead.'
'OK, I'm dead. Now I've risen from the grave and I'm invincible and I'm going to kill you.'
'Oh, fuck off.'

ex-eeeees! What you must shout immediately after you have been tagged in a game of 'it', to indicate that your being tagged was invalid, as you had CLEARLY crossed your fingers, thus exempting yourself from being caught because you were tying your shoelace.

'In reality, a tactic to ensure that Anne-Marie remains "it" for the duration of playtime, despite the number of people she tags. Poor Anne-Marie.'

executive will press for highest penalties against offenders, the A sign on the windows of Isle of Man Transport buses in the 1980s. Easily amended with a 10p piece to *The Executive Will Press His Penis Against Offenders*.

experiment 'Yelled as a preface to fourteen 11-year-old boys wrestling a passer-by to the floor, and stuffing their mouth full of grass. Presumably, because it was an experiment, teachers were loath to interfere, in case they rendered the results useless.'

extreme catshagging 'While most of us sat and watched *Enter the Dragon*, as any non-cat-shagging child would, one of our number went into the next room to play with the cat. After a few moments — long enough — he returned. The *very next day*, our cat gave birth to a litter of kittens. Turning a blind eye to the logic of a human/feline hybrid conceived and born in just 24 hours, this boy became notorious as the man who fathered a litter of kittens.'
See also: catshagging

F f

fainites Also *feighknights*, *keys up*, *quitsies*, *skinchies*. By crossing your fingers and shouting this, you were temporarily immune from all violence or attack. Historically, English soldiers would say it to Nazis in order to allow time to tie up their shoelaces.

As always, *double fainites* are exactly twice as effective.

fake swearing Consequence-free rudeness. Instead of offering the vulgar middle finger, simply extending the ring finger. All the instant shock of the genuine bird, yet unpunishable in a court of law. The parent or teacher will find themselves impotent in the face of your devilish wit.

This also works with swear words; consider *bull sheet*, *bar steward*, *shhhh...ugar*.

There are, of course, those swear words that have a legitimate meaning — *bastard*, *sod*, and so forth. *Twat* became briefly acceptable when the rumour abounded that it meant 'pregnant goldfish'. ***See also: twat***
See also: swear words, permitted

fancy dress Klansmen 'Two children dressed as Ku Klux Klan members, and won second prize in the

Bungay Town Fete. The winner was dressed as a Womble. The fact that the Klansmen outfits came second can only be for very limited reasons. Either the child dressed as a Womble was getting the pity vote because he was retarded, or the judges were well acquainted with proper Klan dress, and couldn't forgive a slight inaccuracy in the gilding around the cuffs.'

fanjo The 'fanny banjo' (famously accompanying the *willy orchestra*) was abbreviated to 'fanjo'. Playing 'air fanjo' was identical to playing air banjo, but with the strumming hand slightly lower than usual.

Not to be confused with the one-stringed willy banjo, or frenum.

fart capacitor A scientific method of storing fart, which – like electricity – is an intangible and mysterious force. If you find yourself with a fart, but with no one suitable to fart on, simply let rip into a cushion. Then, when you meet the first person you care about, hold the cushion to their face, rubbing it around to release the rainbow of fruit flavours.

fart denial, with chins In lieu of '*Whoever smelt it …*' debates, the chin defence could be used. Once the scent of a bumtrump had been smelt, then a clenched fist was attached to the chin. The last person to complete this action was identified as the fart culprit.

Of course, normally the first person to perform the chin defence tended to be the person who had farted – well aware of what they had just done and keen to escape the blame. The loser tended to be anyone who had a bunged up nose or was too absorbed in colouring in the countries of Europe to notice the chinning trend.

This practice also evolved into double chinning, where the second hand should be placed below the first, so you looked like Tutankhamun. Perhaps in ancient Egypt, Tutankhamun got to blame whoever he wanted when he'd gone and done a trump.
See also: whoever smelt it dealt it

farting league

A method of playing football with no ball and two arses.

- **Setting Up**: The two combatants would sit beside each other. Behind them would sit the referee and his assistant.
- **Duration**: A match lasted for a whole lesson. On good days, this could lead to some impressive score lines and the opening of all windows.
- **Scoring**: One goal was awarded for each fart (farts had to be reasonably spaced – a quick follow-up was regarded as a celebratory boot into the back of the net).
- **Fouls**: Any 'fake' fart, whether intended or not, resulted in a penalty. A fake fart could be the player's chair squeaking on the floor, usually followed by the player dramatically protesting his innocence to the ref, or a sinister 'professional foul' kind of fart, executed by the mouth. Or sometimes, while a striker was 'lining up for a shot' but having difficulty 'choosing his spot', he might unintentionally let out a groan or some other verbal effort. These would all result in a penalty.
- **Penalties**: A penalty was taken by impersonating a fart. Easy, either by cupping the hand under the armpit, which resulted in a bit of a top corner net buster, or issuing a simple verbal 'prrrp' through a rattling, curled top lip, which was more of a simple tap-in, with the keeper going the wrong way.
- **Coaching**: As the final approached, unscrupulous 'agents' would try to sell their coaching services, which usually involved little more than them forcing you to get mushy peas with your bag of chips at lunchtime.

farts, special places for

There are certain places where farts are simply funny, no matter what your stance on the humour of atomised turd. In younger years, a finely rounded fart in assembly is, without question, hilarious. In adult years, when applying in the Magistrates' Court for a licence to sell alcohol, a similar enhancement occurs. Even the solicitors smile a bit.

farts, special times for

Holding in a fart can yield great rewards if you release after a key phrase. You don't normally have to wait too long for the right moment – they're everywhere. Consider these everyday situations:

'How do you do?'

(Prap) 'Much better now, thanks.'

'Hello!'

(Prap – look accusingly at own arse)
  'He wasn't talking to YOU!'

'What time is it?'

(Prap) 'Too farty.'

It's almost too easy.

fat boy running

A sight that was both amusing and heartbreaking. Surpassed only by the sight of the fat boy trampolining.

fat brothers

Two children sticking their stomachs out as far as possible can declare themselves to be *the fat brothers*. During their spell as *the fat brothers*, they may form a chorus line or bump their guts into each other, all the while announcing their status as *fat brothers* to an indifferent world.

fat people, why it's ok to be unpleasant to

A thoughtful writer comments:

'It is alright to bully fat people because it's their own fault they eat so much and anyway fat people are supposed to be jolly, and even if they do get angry with the constant aggravation then it's not like they can punch you because for one thing they can barely lift their arms and for another their fingers are so fat it would be like getting assaulted by a cushion so just get over it or stop eating it's your choice for God's sake.'

fatty and thinny

Two subjects of a perpetually expanding song. The pattern of comedy would follow the Little and Large model, wherein Fatty would fart or do something amusing, and Thinny would either suffer, or not be involved. Thinny never got the laughs, and probably fantasised about Fatty's death in many different ways – if my understanding of murder motives is correct.

Sometimes they were friendly:

Fatty and Thinny were in the bath,
Fatty blew off and Thinny laughed.
Sometimes they complemented each other perfectly:
Fatty and Thinny went to the loo,
Fatty did wee wee and Thinny did poo.
And sometimes their adventures seemed like little more than obviously shoehorning a word that rhymes with gay into the first line:
Fatty and Thinny were in the hay,
Fatty blew off and Thinny was gay.
Sometimes Thinny was known as Skinny, and wasn't really involved in the action at all:
Fatty and Skinny went up in a rocket,
Fatty came down with shit in his
pocket.
Fatty and Skinny provided the comedy template for most British double acts in the 70s and 80s.

fatty's reward In the science lab, there are plenty of thievables to hide in the fattest boy's bag. This was especially popular during the fabled time of frog dissection. If done in the last period, there is every chance he will not notice, and take his unwitting booty home with him.

It was imagined that he would get home and dump his bag on the stairs, before running up to his room and leafing through a cook book. His mother would find the hollowed-out frog skins – seemingly picked clean of gizzards by her son's teeth – and shake her head in despair at his monstrous appetite. Then she might give him an extra couple of pounds to spend on sweets, so he didn't have to stop off at the pond for a snack on the way home.

Everyone's a winner with *fatty's reward*.

feef A thief. Also *teef*, as a contraction of the rhyming slang '*tea-leaf*'. Or you could be politically aware, and use '*taxman*'. Because tax is just legal theft, right brothers?

Tax also means 'unauthorised borrowing'. To reclaim something that has been taxed in this way, simply declare Super Tax. There's no such thing as Mega Tax, so if anyone tries *that* on, you can punch them.

felch One of the mythological sex acts which children quoted without entirely understanding. As adults, we all know that it is sucking your own semen out of your partner's anus, and we all do it nearly every day. Then, it was imagined to be a particularly complicated hug.

fenian An Irish Republican. To a certain kind of Belfast Protestant there was no worse insult. Much like *gay*, it became a general word for bad in these circles, so it was no big surprise when a child who had just failed to get the high score on Space Invaders kicked the machine and called it '*Fenian Scum*'.

fiddling As close as one can get to a wank without actually wanking, and therefore becoming a wanker. A fiddle is a practical affair, designed to loosen clammy testicles, or to fix a twisted wicket. It should last no longer than two seconds.

fight fight fight fight
Fight, fight, fight, fight,
Two wee monkeys doing a shite.
Scottish chant, sung during fights. Or perhaps if you see two wee monkeys having a shit, and feel that they are not doing it aggressively enough.

fight room Bog-standard school brutality.

'Basically, the hardest kids in the fourth year would roam the fourth-year rooms in search of likely candidates. Once the victims were selected, they'd be thrown into room D10, and told that they'd get the crap beaten out of them if they didn't fight. Generally, the ensuing violence was so half-hearted that the hard kids got bored and wandered off.'

fireboots
- Spray the tips of the shoes with deodorant for 20 seconds.
- Set the boots alight.
- Frantically kick things and people before the flames go out.

Very briefly became Fireball – the same principle as above but applied to an old Mitre football instead of one's footwear. Briefly, because people started getting hurt.

Combine with the *grundyrunner* for grisly sizzling.

first the worst A song that was sung by people who weren't quite first, and often taken unusually seriously by the person who was first, who in theory shouldn't have anything to prove to the person s/he just beat.

> *First the worst,*
> *second the best,*
> *third the dirty donkey.*

Dirty donkey, also known as hairy princess or the golden eagle. Other versions:

> *First the worst,*
> *second the best,*
> *third the golden eagle,*
> *Fourth the witch, in the ditch,*
> *eating bread and treacle.*

> *First the worst,*
> *second the best,*
> *third the one with the hairy chest,*
> *Fourth the King,*
> *fifth the Queen,*
> *sixth the one in the washing machine.*

In this last version, finishing third is even more desirable than second to boys, so any boy winning a race would stop just before the finish, and wrestle two of his opponents over the line before him. Girls unable to finish in second place would have to slow down and settle for fifth. The sixth position carried no real threat, however, as any cries of *'You're the one in the washing machine'* could be met with the unarguable comeback, *'No, I'm not.'*

And as a final alternative:

> *Fourth the angel,*
> *fifth the ghost,*
> *sixth the one who burnt the toast.*

The implication here seems to be that not possessing rudimentary cooking skills is a fate worse than death.

See also: zero the hero

flamethrower Achieved in the chemistry lab by turning on the gas taps, and igniting them. If you got a few gas taps on the go, this turned a laboratory into a level of *Tomb Raider*.

Attaching the orange Bunsen burner tubes to the gas taps made directional flamethrowers — very good for fights. This does, however, destroy the tubes after a while, so make sure you steal plenty of them.

flea castle A way of defending yourself, should you find yourself sharing a dinner table with a smelly person.

Construct a wall using sandwich boxes, Club biscuits, anything you can lay your hands on. Use drinks bottles or Thermos flasks as watchtowers. Irregular items may find an improvised use — for example, bananas make excellent flea cannons.

flea powder In the absence of proper medical resources, chalk dust was an acceptable replacement for flea powder. Anyone suspected of having fleas would therefore be forced to willingly consent to being attacked with board rubbers, for the good of the class.

flidding Thalidomide was a pill prescribed to pregnant women who suffered from severe morning sick-

ness. A godsend to prospective mothers going through daily cramps and nausea.

There was an enormous stormcloud to this silver lining. The drug, not having undergone sufficient testing, caused the child to be born with missing arms and legs. There was no logic to it; an arm, a leg, both arms, an arm and a leg — the drug seemed to set in motion a grim limb lottery.

As most children's exposure to the victims of Thalidomide was limited to triumph-over-adversity features on *John Craven's Newsround*, it was down to them to emulate their own missing limbs, which they did by retracting their arms into their coats or pressing their wrists against their sides, and running around in little circles. Or into walls. This practice was known as *flidding*.

fog, the Book by James Herbert and most people's first experience of breathtakingly, eye-poppingly, gob-smackingly, hardcore pornography. If you are 11.

The Fog could be read in public with total impunity, as its cover in no way belied the graphic, frank depictions of adult lovemaking that could be found within.

The only problem with *The Fog* was Herbert's use of sex as metaphor. Herbert explores the idea of sex as celebration of life, with death as the great disclosure, revealing the loneliness and horror of life's seedy underbelly with the literary device of contrast. ('In the midst of life we are in death', and so on.) To demonstrate life's rich tapestry of light and dark, pleasures and woes, sex is used to throw death into sharp relief, and vice versa.

This means that just as a sex scene was getting to the really filthy bit, the character would chop off their own cock with a pair of gardening shears, or throw themselves into the sea on top of a load of corpses after a big lezzing session.

Most psychosexual dysfunctions can be attributed to early childhood exposure to *The Fog*.

foot chuffers 'The essence of foot chuffers is to stamp on the opponent's foot. To do so is to score a chuff. However, to prevent random unprovoked stampings, a series of gentlemanly procedures were developed, regarding a signing on and off process.

'To sign on, both combatants must raise their right leg and declare the commencement of foot chuffing. Players then remain in a state of war until one player signs off. Initially, a mutual and simultaneous signing off was required, in the same fashion of the signing on. However, some warriors would refuse to sign off, and carry on stamping on their opponent's feet for days after, sometimes weeks. After much injustice, the constitutional amendment was passed to allow unilateral signings off.

'Special moves include the reverse chuff (heel on toe), the double chuff, and the total chuff combo (a reverse double chuff). Exotic moves, which were never put into practice, were the flip chuff, the uberchuff, and ETERNAL NIGHT.'

franzi the gay pig Franzi was a cartoon pig in *Deutsche Heut* textbooks who always seemed to be a few penstrokes away from a lewd sexual act. Even when he wasn't, you could always just draw a speech bubble and make him say 'I love cock'. That crazy gay pig.

freddy fish finger A way of getting cheap thrills. Two eyes are drawn on the index finger, which is then passed under the hem of a tasty teacher's skirt while she is close by, but facing the other way. What Freddy 'sees' with his inky eyes is transmitted to his master, causing him to jolt into a dramatic fake orgasm.

freemealers, the Term of abuse aimed at children of unemployed alcoholic parents living on council estates. In the early 70s there was a kids' adventure serial, screened pre-teatime, called *The Freewheelers*. Anybody who was subject to free dinners was thereafter known as a *Freemealer*.

frigidity test An imperfect method of coercing girls into vague sexual acts. Accusing them of frigidity would generally result in a denial, whereupon you would be perfectly within your rights asking them to prove it. If she agreed then you got to feel her ladybumps while she stood as still as she could. Most girls would usually tell you to piss off, though.

frog blowing Get a thin drinking straw from a Calypso packet. Catch a frog. Spawning season is a good time, as they're too busy clambering all over each other to bother about having a thin straw stuck up their anus. Stick the thin straw up the frog's anus. Blow gently. Believe it or not, this inflates the frog, which cannot then deflate.
Warning: THIS ENTRY IS AN UTTER LIE.

frottage When queuing to get into classrooms, there tended to be a certain degree of pushing. This pushing is similar to the sexual act of frotting. Anyone being so pushed may commentate – *'frot frot frot'* – or accuse –

'*frotter!*' – or just be squealingly camp – '*Oh goodie, frottage.*'

fub A *fat useless bastard*. Simply being fat was not enough. You had to be useless, as well. For girls, *fat useless bitch*.

fuck The game of fuck is good fun for two or more players. It is best played in a classroom, but also works in the playground, as long as a teacher is nearby. The first player says 'fuck' very quietly. The next player has to say it a little louder, and so on around the players. The loser is the first person to say 'fuck' more quietly than the previous person, to bottle out completely, or to be heard by the teacher.

There is a variant of fuck called '*anal fist fuck*', with remarkably similar rules, and sterner punishments.

'For the advanced fucker, there is a more dangerous version, very rarely played. You hold your hand in the air, middle finger extended, and say loudly "one motherfucker". The next person says "one, two motherfucker" and so on. I never knew it get higher than five motherfucker, and we eventually had a year assembly warning us that if it happened again, expulsion would follow.'

A final variant on the fuck theme is dropping the word 'fuck' into the middle of a normal sentence. In the following example, when the teacher expressed surprise the player had to repeat the sentence with 'fuck' removed:

Ben: And you can tell the church was built at the same time, cos it's got all them fuckin' crenellations along the top.

Mrs Whittaker: What did you say?

Ben: I said, it's got all those crenellations along the top. Y'know, like on the castle.

fuck fuck willy willy wank wank piss
See: fuck shit wanker tit bum

fucking egg, well this is like talking to a
Retort to a bald teacher who claims that teaching you is like 'talking to a wall'.

fuck shit wanker tit bum This phrase can be used in a face-to-face argument (provided that swearing is still seen as naughty), or simply as a curse. It has to be said quickly and with passion to be effective, but you can't help thinking that it would be even more effective and grown-up if it didn't end with 'tit' and 'bum'.

fucktion A poor attempt on the part of a teacher to hide an unmistakable swear.

'The pause between the *fuck* and the *shun* was far too long. Rumours went around for six weeks that she was being sent to teach in the Congo, which is what happens to teachers who do swears.'

furtle A furtive fondle. A form of intimacy popular amongst turtles.

fuzzy duck A well-known game where people say *fuzzy duck* in a circle, until someone says *does he?*, after which people must say *ducky fuzz*, the idea being that you get free swears, most often *does he fuck*, or *fuck he does*.

At a certain age, alcohol is added to this game to make it seem less, well, rubbish. Or more rubbish, considering that you are old enough to be drinking alcohol, and should really be able to say fuck whenever you like.

G g

gary lineker makes my tits erect 'Scrawled into the desk at which I sat my Italian GCSE. Hopefully the work of a misguided lady, rather than an overweight boy with arousable breasts.'

gas van attack 'The sighting of a British Gas van would initiate the pummelling of a random child. The only protection from becoming the victim of a *gas van attack* was to shout "*Gas van no rebounds*" at the top of your voice. British Gas van drivers in areas where this game was popular probably had quite a bleak view of humanity's future, witnessing a near-constant stream of mindless violence.'

gay 1. Stupid, bad, wrong, funny peculiar, boring, unfashionable, irritating. Rubbish. '*Your shoes are gay.*' **2.** (obsolete) Homosexual.

gay barry Standard insult. Sometimes lengthened to Gay Barry Bender. Occasionally Gay Barry Bender on the Bumbus. The Bumbus ran a shuttle service from Willyville to Shittham Hall.

gay games The **GAY-me** (pronounced game) A game in which you define how gay someone is by the things that they like most in the world.

You are so gay, your favourite ...

* singer is Marvin GAYe
* TV show is *GAYme for a Laugh*
* children's book is *Anne of Green GAYbles*
* composer is SerGAY Prokofiev (pronounced 'Sir Gay', also has the bonus of tying in nicely with *Gaylord*).

The game ends when someone says something that gay people actually do like, such as 'I Will Survive' by Gloria GAYnor, the *GAY Times*, or GAY sex.

gay humour An all-purpose comeback: *'Is that gay humour? I don't understand it because I'm not gay.'*

gaymo Insult currently in use amongst 5-6 year olds. They simply like the sound of it, and are probably not even aware that it is a highly sophisticated conjunction of the words 'gay' and 'Flymo'.

gay pub 'At some point in everyone's life, they will become aware that some pubs are *gay pubs*. Pubs for real gay people, to be gay in. Before gay people became less embarrassed about what they got up to and started being gay on telly and everything, these bars would generally have blacked-out windows, and in some cases have a tiny slot window on the front door, like a Prohibition speak-easy. This invisibility lent them a terrifying mystique. It was common to dare a friend to run inside the pub and retrieve a trophy, such as a real gay beer mat. It was believed that this would trigger a reaction similar to that of bombing a chicken shed, and that the child would run out, followed by a burst of feathers and glitter. Annoyingly, this didn't happen.

'Interestingly enough, gay pubs of long-standing are often used as part of an insult. *"We'll be seeing you down The Jester if you don't cut that hair"* would be used in Birmingham, for example, by a father who disapproves of his son's girlish footballer's hair. These pubs are rarely the fashionable pubs; your dad knows about them, for God's sake. So *don't go to these pubs to get your first gay experience*. You will find yourself surrounded by decrepit mingers, and may end up going into 10 years of denial.'

gay raper A name you might like to consider should you ever meet anyone called Guy Roper.

gay showers Shower cubicles that had a solid door, preventing access and prying glances, were sturdy heterosexual showers. Those showers with a flimsy curtain, which allowed young gayers-in-training to stare (as the users of the heterosexual showers imagined) at their soapy nuts, were the gay showers.
'Why don't you use the gay showers?'
'Because they're gay.'

gay tray A common badge of gayness in the school canteen.
'All of the trays in our canteen were dark brown wood except one, which was slightly lighter. This became the gay tray, and if it was top of the pile when you came to the stack, you were

obliged to use it. This usually meant for a dinner hour of isolation and ridicule. Taking the normal, presumably straight, tray from underneath it was even worse. You were then 'gay scared' (a kind of state of beyond gayness) and received a beating behind the stage curtains. One boy got set up with the gay tray every day for a week, until he was caught throwing it into the skip during break. The preferred interpretation of this event was that he was on a secret date with the gay tray.'

g.b.h. Part of the continuing efforts to render teachers impotent in the face of increasingly savvy children. It rapidly became widespread knowledge that teachers would get sacked if they struck a child.

So, even the lightest touch on the most savage of bullies would be met with hollers of 'Aaaarrr, G.B.H.! That's G.B.H. sir!' followed by a chant of 'G! – B! – H!' The teacher would then be forced into a meek retreat or genuine G.B.H.

This is possibly why Morrissey went from singing about evil headmasters in The Smiths' 'The Headmaster Ritual' to declaring 'The Teachers Are Afraid Of The Children' on his *Southpaw Grammar* album. That and the fact he got old, and shit.

G.b.S. Greasy bum sex. When you ask someone if they like *G.B.S.*, you should do so in front of their closest friends and family. The conversation generally follows this pattern:

A: Do you like G.B.S.?

B: What's G.B.S.?

A: Do you like it? Everyone else does. It's great!

B: But what is it?

A: Just say you like it. Say you like G.B.S.

B: No. Tell me what it is.

A: I will if you say you like it.

B: OK … I like G.B.S.

A: Aha! You like *greasy bum sex*.

Now, everyone in the room knows that Child B enjoys greasy bum sex on a regular basis. Even his parents, who are shocked and disappointed at their son's hitherto secret fetish.

'*You could have told us first … we wouldn't have minded. But not like this! Not in front of all these people!*'

genital interrogation

One day, between the ages of six and nine, someone will learn the proper name for willies and fanjos. They will use this knowledge to run around all day saying, 'Have you got a penis or a vagina?'

Your reply, if based on guesswork, will be met with howls of derision if you get it wrong, and a begrudging 'Errr, yeah, you have, actually' if you get it right.

This is how most people learn the words 'penis' and 'vagina'.

genital reassignment

In much the same way that some circumcised men reclaim their foreskin, it seems fair that pupils should correct glaring biological omissions in textbooks, especially regarding the absence of big hairy cocks. They may even be included on drawings of fully clothed men. Hell, draw them on fully clothed women, if you like.

Bonus points if there is someone in the background with a surprised look on their face.

german terrorists, we are

'A lunchtime mission based on the similarity of the words "tourists" and "terrorists". A polite German couple, asking some patriotic children for directions to a place of no political importance, suddenly found themselves being chased down the street, and having stones thrown at their heads.'

getting insults wrong

Not guaranteed, but satisfying when it works. The insultee may correct the insult, thus confirming and accepting it.

Person A: 'You're a fuckwick.'

Person B: 'Fuckwick? You mean fuckwit.'

Person A: 'Yeah, that's what you are, thanks.'

ghost gang, the

A gang formed in response to the rumour that a school was haunted. The activities of *The Ghost Gang,* however, were not confined to capturing or investigating ghosts. In fact, once it was established that ghosts were quite difficult to find, it was agreed that diabetics, vegetarians and asthmatics would be hunted instead.

gippo box

The lost-property box in games, full of spare clothes. This is used by three sets of people:

- fat or feeble kids who wilfully forget their kit to avoid games;
- trevors who can't afford their own kit;
- normal children who simply forgot it was games (these are perhaps the most unfortunate group; because the *gippo box* is never laundered, the poor normal child will be forced to run around in fat kids' bollock sweat and poor kids' fleas).

girls acting like horses

A more common practice than most recall. Girls would harness each other with skipping ropes and canter around the playground. Some girls would even bring riding crops in, smacking themselves on the arse as they jumped over small obstacles, in a display that has led to nearly all modern bondage fantasy. Even poorer girls who couldn't afford horses would own a riding crop with which to spank themselves.

Cartoonist John Willie developed this horsey instinct to a fine degree in his work; fans of women acting like horses would be well recommended to read *The Adventures of Gwendoline*.

glass eyes The mythology and curiosity surrounding glass eyes (Are they easily removed? Do they fly out if you sneeze? Can you spin them around really fast?) is entirely natural, but can be abused.

'Our youth group had two leaders who didn't get along. One leader confided to all of us that the other leader had a glass eye; if we snuck up behind her and hit her in the back of the head it would fall out. He considerately told us not to tell her he'd told us, because she was very sensitive about it.

'The fact that she would be upset by us mentioning her glass eye but not by hordes of children punching her in the back of the head seemed perfectly reasonable to us. Of course she didn't have a glass eye, it didn't fall out, and so we simply kept trying.'

See also: ten pence

glory, glory, hallelujah

Glory, glory, hallelujah,
Teacher hit me with a ruler.
So I punched her in the belly,
And she wobbled like a jelly,
And she hopped like a kangaroo.

A good example of children getting bored at the end of a song and just saying anything for the fucking sake of it.

goat's cheese During lessons, or lunch break in the canteen, someone may shout 'Goat's Cheese'. As a matter of fierce pride all the lads in the room have to stop whatever they're doing, rest their chins upon the table and then, by wiggling it, 'walk' their chin across the table. The first person to achieve this feat would get a round of applause before carrying on as normal. Given the amiably harmless futility of this exercise, the punishment of a beating for not taking part is unjustifiably extreme.

go buy one A pithy annoyance that everyone said for a week. This is the general format:

'Would you like a crisp?' (packet offered)

'Ooh, ta.'

'Go buy one.' (packet casually withdrawn)

The acceptability of the phrase lasts for a week or two, after which it will have 'gone out with the dinosaurs'.

See also: charity week; nothing

go to Say you were on page 76 in your textbook, trying to work through a tricky problem. Then you saw that someone had written 'go to page 15' in the corner. What's on page 15? Something must be pretty good on page 15 for someone to deface school property to tell you about it. So you turned to page 15, and there it was: 'go to page 168'. So you follow the signposts back and forth, hither and yon,

through topics covered and topics yet to be learned, always aware that you could be busted by the teacher at any time for being on the wrong page.

At the end of the journey is either a drawing of some tits (jackpot!), a drawing of a cock (more jackpot!) or the words 'gayers flick through books' (ha ha ha). Alternatively, you could get directed back to page 76.

god, being your own Take a Philips school atlas and find where you live on it. Show your friends what you're about to do. Bring your thumb down on your home town, and you should hear all your mates screaming with terror as a 50-mile-wide thumb descends upon them and crushes them like red mites. Gob on the map, and hear them choke and drown.

Best of all, turn round and fart all over the East Midlands.

god's hatred God is an all-powerful being. Everything that happens in the world is within his control and jurisdiction. To the simple mind of the adorable child, unaware of God's 2,000-year policy of non-intervention, any misfortune that befalls a person must happen simply because God hates that person.

This concept can lead to some staggeringly unsympathetic comments, in particular when applied to a child whose mother has just been killed in a car crash.

going into orbit

Directed at a fat child. Any number of children would start running around him in circles, begging, 'Help, I'm trapped in your gravity field! I'm going into orbit!'

The game would continue until the entire class was stuck to a grumpy fat boy.

golden cockerel infinite regress

The best minds of a generation were destroyed by the *Golden Cockerel Hymn Book*, on the cover of which was a photo of a few kids singing merrily and holding copies of the *Golden Cockerel Hymn Book*, on the cover of which was a photo of a few kids singing merrily and holding copies of the *Golden Cockerel Hymn Book*.

Pupils who had seen the *Twilight Zone* lived in constant fear of turning their heads around quickly enough to see their own huge face glaring down at them.

gold watches

An alternative name for *skid marks*. Based on the defence of one luckless fat child, who responded to allegations of skidders with: '*Shut up! My dad says they're called gold watches, and they're good luck!*'

The strange relationship this child had with his father – in which *skid marks* were discussed in a positive light – suddenly became the least of his worries.

goof troop, the

Any two big-teethed individuals who are stupid enough to hang around together, or even be seen together at any point. Named after the mildly popular Disney cartoon series.

A useful message therefore for people who are different. To avoid such

insults as 'Goof Troop', or 'Elmo Putney's Wine Bar', try not to be best friends with someone who is different in the same way as yourself. Try to get a gang with a fat one, a clever one, a spotty one. Then ride around on your bikes (unless you're the fat kid, in which case turn up everywhere 20 seconds late and out of breath), find a treasure map, and solve mysteries.
See also: elmo

goose milk 'This was the name I unwittingly coined for a kind of prototype Nesquik pink milkshake which was occasionally foisted on us at primary school in place of a proper pudding. As we all suspiciously sniffed and sipped it upon its debut appearance, I declared that it tasted like goose milk – my uncle was a farmer so everyone reckoned I must be an expert in such matters. This scandal soon reached the ears of Alison Beaumont's mum, a renowned busybody who promptly wrote to the headmistress to point out that goose milk was no fit beverage for growing children.'

granny bashing The tabloid phenomenon of granny bashing caught the imaginations of many a child, because the words sounded so cute and harmless together. Children would run around, often with their jumpers over their heads, declaring themselves to be granny bashers.

granny's garden An early educational computer game, used in schools to promote learning without human interaction. The initial opening, as with all games, usually ran like this...
Hello, what is your name?
> FUCK
What do you want to do now, FUCK?
> Yes please
... after which you would be subjected to a series of puzzles. Such as finding a house with the word FIG painted on the side ...
There is a secret word on the house. Do you know what it is?
> Knob
No, that's not it.
> Cock

No, the word is on the house in big blue letters.

> Shit

No, the word is FIG.

> Bum

No, the word is FIG.

Free will has always been stifled in children, as a matter of guidance and protection. Granny's Garden echoed this admirably:

Can you see a cave?

> no

Yes you can. Do you want to go into the cave?

> no

Yes you do.

A triumph of interactivity.

grapple my grapenuts

'Derived from Lenny Henry's impersonation of David Bellamy. Obviously, when he said "grapple my grapenuts", he was trying to make it sound like it meant "twist my bollocks". That was the joke, you see. Our school, however, put the translation into agonising practice.

'And yet strangely, it was quite charming to have your balls crushed by someone who was making the effort to entertain.'

great sage, the An amazing game allowing one boy the most power he will ever have.

'The rules were simple. I would sit cross-legged on the grass waving a twig around while my huge overweight followers would ask, "What is your will, Great Sage?" Usually my will involved beating up smaller followers, although occasionally I would send one of my followers to buy me a can of Coke.

'Looking back it is quite disturbing to think I derived so much pleasure from sitting back watching kids beaten up purely because I had asked for it to be done. Mind, this is probably the only real power I ever had, and I doubt whether I will experience its like again.'

green wee man 'Our school had blue urinals. Thus, if you were standing next to someone you didn't like, you could accuse them of being the Green Wee Man. Reversal etiquette prevented

your defendant from pointing out that your wee was green, too.

'Once challenged, the victim may be called upon to piss outside, to prove that his wee wasn't green. Whether he failed or passed this test was down to the whim of his peers, rather than any serious reference to a colour chart. Some chose to accept the obviously false rumour of having green wee rather than produce their penis and urinate for the benefit of a crowd of braying boys. The gay.'

grundyrunner One who runs around with shit-encrusted shoes, with the intention of daubing someone else with it. The name applies to both the game and the prominent participant of the game. Can be combined with *fireboots* to create a sizzling atrocity.
See also: fireboots

guess the hair Whilst in detention a group of boys could play 'guess the hair', which is not really a game, as much as pulling out a handful of pubes and putting them on each other's books. There was no winner. Maybe everyone was a winner.

guess what? For 11-16s, you had:
A : Guess what?
B : What?
A : Good guess.
For under 10s, something a little more basic was required:
A. Guess what?
B. What?
A. Hotpot.
A. Guess why?
B. Why?
A. Pork pie.
On reflection it's a little disappointing that we never utilised when, where, how or who. Especially who, because that rhymes with poo.

gullibility, abuse of If you know someone gullible, these are just a few of the things they have probably believed in their time:
● The new boy's name is Gerard Depardieu;
● The new girl is the girl from off the test card;

- That kid's uncle's hand operates Edd the Duck;
- A really cool way to say 'hello' to a French Exchange student is 'Fromage Frais';
- Both of their parents are dead.

gush, the 'Trying to laugh without making a noise is an under-recognised and difficult art, much like referees running backwards. For one child, when told the colour of a female classmate's underwear, the effort to keep in the laughter was too much. The grunt that finally escaped would have had a West Country swineherd dropping his teacup in shock.

'The visual results were also extraordinary; the poor child was clearly ill. Layer upon layer of creamy green goodness, dispensed from a nostril into his cupped hands like so much Mr Whippy, before the poor sod was escorted from the class to see the nurse. All around him was wonderment and disbelief.'

gypsy's challenge A game derived from the rhyming slang of *gypsy's kiss*, meaning piss. Quite simply, drink four cans of Coke and the last one to take a slash wins.

gypsy's kiss This time, not related to the rhyming slang for piss. This *gypsy's kiss* is the art of farting into your clenched hand before releasing the fumes into the unsuspecting victim's face. To attain the full effect, you have to whisper '*gypsy's kisssss*' as you do so. This is probably racist, but then so is *eenie meenie minie mo*.
See also: eenie meenie minie mo

Hh

hacking When the film *War Games* came out in 1983, a generation of children became dimly aware of what computers could do. By 1984, everyone knew someone who had sent 500 tanks into Russia and had the FBI around their house telling them off for it.

If you are American, you could use *hacking* to amend your grades on that pop quiz you just like totally failed, provided you knew the name of the principal's cat. That'd be the password.

haircut 100 A semi-popular band of the 80s. Said to any child arriving at school with a severe haircut. The number rises if the haircut is particularly savage, or ridiculous.

You rarely heard a haircut in excess of Haircut 1000, which is somewhat reserved to say that children use 'babwillions' to mean any number greater than 50.

haircut city 'The city in which *Puddingbowl Lane* is the high street. Based on a mid-80s advert for 'Carpet City', in which the voiceover man was pondering his whereabouts. He knew he was in some kind of city ... but which city was beyond him. As rolls of carpets enveloped his vision, this voiceover man would ask "New York City?"

'Sensing that he wasn't right, the voiceover man would walk down endless aisles of carpets, with an increasing edge of panic in his voice. "Mexico City ...?" he would offer waveringly.

'Luckily, a cartoon squirrel thing was at hand to put him right. "No, it's Carpet City!" the squirrel would announce in a nasal whine, as it swept inexpensively across the screen.

'So, if you see someone with a severe haircut, another option open to you is for two people to re-enact this advert, but scream *"No, it's HAIRCUT City!"* at the end, as you both launch yourself at the head of the cropped child.'

hairlo Said instead of 'Hello' as you approach someone who has had a particularly noticeable haircut. Only really funny when a whole group of people hear and understand, and the unwitting recipient just dumbly replied 'All right, mate'.

hairy balls theorem A bonus branch of mathematics not generally taught in most A Level courses. To be taught this topic, you simply write 'TODAY: HAIRY BALLS THEOREM' on the blackboard before the teacher enters, and as they wearily start to rub it out, insist firmly that you were promised Hairy Balls Theorem, and Hairy Balls Theorem is all you wish to learn.

half-mast 'Put some jam on your shoes and invite your trousers down for tea.'

A pair of trousers that leave too much sock visible. Indicative that your family's clothing budget does not stretch to accommodate human growth, or that you are so poor you have to wear your younger brother's hand-me-ups.

hallowed be thy ... If you could fart in the small gap between 'thy' and 'name' during an assembly recital of the Lord's Prayer, you would win the kudos jackpot and be immune from all forms of unpleasantness for the rest of your life.

See also: farts, special times for

hand, cancer diagnosis

The victim is informed that new medical research has found a genetic link between the size of your hands and the probability of developing cancer in later life. The details of the research are obviously very complicated, but it boils down to a simple rule of thumb; if your hand is bigger than your face, then you're very likely to develop cancer. The curious victim will immediately check by placing their hand against their nose, allowing you to push their palm hard into their face.

This is actually very painful, and runs the risk of hitting the *Kung-Fu death spot*, which shoots the nose backwards into the brain.

hand man

Invite someone to shake the hand of a little invisible man standing on your hand. When they do, look aghast and say, 'That wasn't his *hand.*'

happiness or half an e?

Another trick based on getting boys to say they are girls (eur!) or girls to say they are boys (yuck!). The subject is asked, 'Were you born with happiness or half an e?'

More often than not, a boy trying to sound drugswise will reply, 'Half an e,' to which you reply, 'Ha ha, you just said you were born with a fanny!' Girls, being in tune with their emotions like they are, reply 'happiness', which of course sounds like 'a penis'. Haa … penis!

harvey wallbangers

A method of inducing a faint. Child A stands with his back to the wall and breathes as deeply and quickly as possible. Child B observes. Once close to hyperventilation, Child A exhales completely, and Child B presses his chest firmly against the wall. As if by magic, Child A faints, slumping to the floor. It is generally good practice to insist that you nearly died, and that you definitely saw the light that time.

have you got a rubber, jonny?

If a classroom contained a child called Jonathan or John, all requests for rubbers would be directed at him, even from people on the other side of the room. 'Jonny' might stop bringing rubbers to school – that would not stop the requests. In fact, when Jonny needed a rubber himself, he would have to ask for one, and people would say, 'What, haven't you got a rubber, Jonny?'

head bagging

A practice worthy of any Guy Ritchie movie.

'Exceptionally large holdalls manufactured by Head were briefly fashionable in the late 1980s and early 1990s. From their "classic" look – a base blue colour with red lettering – the bags became so popular that they started making pink bags for girls, and fluorescent ones for wankers.

'The inside of a Head Bag was so vast that nobody could hope to fill it with legitimate school supplies, but it *was* the perfect size for us to incarcerate any first-year pupil who happened to own one. A twist of a paperclip would lock the zip, and a good kicking would be applied for luck. After lunch it was common to see at least one squirming body bag in the middle of the playground.'

headmistress, shagging the

'At the tender age of 11, several boys in my year decided that because I was so clever, I must be shagging the headmistress. I pointed out that if this accusation were true, then I must have developed sexually much more rapidly than them. So I was both more intelligent, and more physically mature than my accusers, and should be looked up to.

'I got punched. For ending a sentence with a preposition, I should imagine.'

head open, he's split his

A lie used to make a bleeding face seem more exciting. If you hear someone shouting, '*He's split his head open*,' the odds are you're not going to see brains. Sorry about that.

health hazard

After looking at pictures of the 'unsafe kitchen', and

identifying all the health hazards, pupils became particularly keen on spotting such hazards in everyday life. Anyone leaving their bag on the floor would be met with a parade of other children elaborately tripping over it, and declaring, 'HEALTH HAZARD!'

This is the precursor to the idea that everyone had, one year later, of spilling milk in the local supermarket, slipping in it and breaking their leg. Then suing the supermarket for a million and one pounds. *See illustration overleaf.*

heats A variation on *beats*. A comb, usually plastic, would be heated with a lighter and then combed through the victim's hair, who would have a burnt scalp and crappy lumps of melted plastic stuck in his hair.

A female victim *might* be convinced to participate willingly in this game, if you convinced her that it was how Floella Benjamin did her hair.

See also: beats

hedge hopping One of the few practices that will actually get home-owners into their front gardens and shaking their fists at a group of unruly children. Works best with a row of semi-detached houses with goodish sized gardens, or at the back of terraced housing if you fancy a wall-climbing challenge.

Hedge hopping could be combined with *rosebudding* (throwing rosebuds at windows), and *ghostknocking/ Knock Down Ginger* (knocking on a door and running away), to form the ultimate in residential carpet-bombing.

hello sailor! Inform a friend that they have something on the back of their shoe. When they twist round and kick their leg upwards behind them to see, say, 'Ooh, hello sailor!'

hello sir, it's paul allen What not to say when making a prank phone call to a teacher, and your name is Paul Allen.

hiding in a cupboard and mooing One of the many millions of ways to make religious education

The unsafe kitchen

1. Marbles on floor — slipping hazard.

2. Dangling kettle wire.

3. Overloaded socket and frayed cable.

4. Pan on hob contains poison.

5. Beachball over the biscuit tins.

6. An angry bear is wielding a large sword in front of the cutlery drawer.

less tedious, along with using red pen on the palms of your hands and screaming '*stigmata*'.

See also: circumcision, what is?

hitler baby The textbook used for GCSE history's 'Rise of the Nazis' featured, on the very first page, a picture of Adolf Hitler as a baby. This taught us that even genocidal warmongers have an innocent history, and made us think more introspectively on the nature of innate and learned evil.

Anyway, they all got moustaches drawn on them. Even by the girls. It was impossible to see that baby and not draw a moustache on it. *See illustration.*

hobnob gobbler As ugly as a hobgoblin? Eat too many biscuits? Love gobbling nobs? Then this is the versatile word for you.

holmes ejaculated Conan Doyle's unfortunate way of saying that Sherlock Holmes had said something with emphasis. When reading the books in class, these words were to be uttered with sudden loudness during a dreary reading in English class.

It's not all ejaculating, though. In *A Case of Identity*, a lady clearly upset by the criminal goings-on 'pulled a little handkerchief out of her muff, and began to sob heavily into it'. One of Holmes' bolder ejaculations even had a lady returning her hands to her muff in disgust.

A Terribly Strange Bed by Wilkie Collins contains the line, 'He solemnly ejaculated "coffee!"' Additionally, Shakespeare's *Macbeth* abuses his position of power to ask Banquo, 'Ride you this afternoon?' to which Banquo wearily replies, 'Ay, my good Lord.' You could imagine Banquo rolling his eyes and thinking, 'Here we go again.'

horace The name of a Christian puppet who toured West Country primary school assemblies, in a suitcase.

'He was carried by a variety of human "hosts", most notably a portly woman named Dawn. Every year, Horace would emerge sleepily from the suitcase and crack the same joke about thinking he was at a zoo, on

hitler Baby

Hitler, as he might appear without his trademark moustache. Before you fill in the moustache yourself, why don't you consider adding the Tom Selleck, the Salvador Dali, or the Bill Oddie? We have included a second Hitler for your experimentation.

87

account of all the monkeys present. After making a number of observations about how a number of things were "a bit like Jesus, really", it was customary for Dawn to pack Horace away, pretending to shut his legs in the suitcase as she did so. It was about this time I stopped attending Sunday School.'

huey lewis Where your attitude is marked as G, S, or U (Good, Satisfactory, or Unsatisfactory), and your achievement is ranked from A to E, the best possible grade was G-A. The insults for clever, well-behaved — well, gay — children was therefore obvious. However, to attain the ultimate in unruly stupidity, a 'U-E Lewis' was a badge of honour for some.

hulla mulla The cry of The Bumblers.

'The Bumblers spoke in a high, loud voice and said "Hulla Mulla". You may think that The Bumblers sounds like a popular television show for children. Sadly, it wasn't. They — or rather, he — went to my school.'

hymns, replacing words in

- **While Shepherds Watched Their Flocks By Night**
  While shepherds washed
  their cocks at night,
  While watching BBC,
  The angel of the Lord came down
  And switched to ITV.

- **The Lord's Prayer**
  Our Father, who aren't in Heaven,
  Hello! What's your name?

- **Come Let Us Adore Him**
  Come let us ignore him ...
  Christ! I'm bored.

- **Peace Is Flowing Like A River**
  Piss is flowing like a river,
  Flowing out of you and me.

- **Cross Over The Road**
  Cross over the road my friend,
  Ask the Lord his cock to bend,
  Hi-is penis knows no end,
  Cross over the road.

- **Jesus Christ The Apple Tree**
  JESUS CHRIST! The APPLE TREE!

- **We Three Kings**
  We three kings of Leicester Square,
  Selling ladies' underwear,
  No elastic, how fantastic,
  Now all your bums are bare.

I i

i am a robot The heartbreaking defence mechanism of one child to his daily tauntings. He would simply fend off all verbal and physical attacks by adopting a monotone voice and saying, '*I am a robot. You cannot hurt me.*'

This was in stark contrast to the fact that he wasn't, and we could.

i blue off

Kid A: What's the ninth letter of the alphabet?
Kid B (pause while fingers are counted on): I.
Kid A: What colour is the sky?
Kid B: Blue.
Kid A: What's the opposite of on?
Kid B: Off.
Kid A: Euuuurrrrr! You blew off!
You blew off! Hey everyone, [Kid A] just said 'I blew off'!
This joke is best suited to the under 10s or the over- 30s.

i now have the honour of eating a potato A remarkably polite ceremony during which a roast potato would be held up on a fork, and stuffed whole into the mouth after declaring that it was your honour to do so. The potato would be so hot as to cause steam to shoot out of the ears, but it was impolite and ungrateful to look pained or spit out the potato; it was, after all, your very great honour to be eating it in the first place.

i should be so lucky ...

Alternative lyrics of Kylie's debut single.

I should be so lucky
with my rubber ducky,
Strangle Mrs Mangle today.
Daphne's had a baby,
Called it little Jamie;
Bouncer's gone a bouncing away.

Seeing as the song stuck so fastidiously to the plotlines of 1980s *Neighbours*, it is let down somewhat by the addition of the rubber ducky, which robs the song of its impact and gravitas. Could try harder. See me.

i take plastic

'As a follow-up to a witty one-liner, I *intended* this to mean, 'What I just said was excellent — I'll accept your appreciative donations via credit card.' My classmates, however, interpreted it as an admission that I liked to stick dildos up my bum. My victory was short-lived.'

i'm an alley cat!

'Two kids had been caught fighting. In next day's assembly, our headmaster made a dramatic speech. He got rather worked up, and offered us the following:

'"*So anyone who wants to fight in the future, fight me! I know the alley! I've fought in the alleys! I'm an alley cat!*"

'These ludicrous threats were heard out in stunned silence, only to be much analysed, mused upon and repeated in the following months.'

i'm not gay!

To say '*I'm not gay*' is the highest, most solemn, most utterly damning evidence that one *is* gay, and not just gay but a big brassy transvestite to boot. The quickest, kindest cure for this was to kick the victim.

i'm sofa king we tar did

Which, when written on a piece of paper and read out by someone else, sounds quite funny.

i've been hit in the willy

What you say before you are old enough to know that it's your *spas-*

mojesticles that hurt when you get hit in them. Although being kicked in the willy does make your pipe hot for a bit.

i've lost my puberty! The
slightly confused announcement made in Year 8 by a child who had just pretended to shag a chain-link fence.

ib dib dog shit Another it-select-
ing rhyme:

Ib dib dog shit,
Fucking bastard,
Dirty git
... [continue swearing] ...
You are not IT!

After the third line, the lyrics were vari-able and usually consisted of the picker reciting as many other swear words as they could think of until they ran out. This also allowed them to cheat, by timing the swear words to stop four before the one they wanted out, but no one really noticed that because they were too busy listening to loads of cool swear words.

The rhyme improved with the age of the rhymer, until eventually the selection process aspect of the rhyme was lost in a purposeless stream of filth.

iced ink 'If you put water in the
freezer you get iced water. What do you get if you put ink in the freezer?' 'Iced ink.' 'Yes, you do stink! Ha ha ha!'

Double bluff possible: reply 'frozen ink'. The other person may (a 1:25 chance) say, 'No, iced ink,' allowing you full reversal privileges.

ich habe hunger A German
song, featured in the *Deutsch Heut* book. Translated literally ...

I am hungry, hungry, hungry,
I am hungry, hungry, hungry,
I am hungry, hungry, hungry,
I am thirsty.
Where is the food, food, food
Where is the food, food, food
Where is the food, food, food
Where is the sausage?

Nice of the Germans to stereotype themselves so effectively, and saving other countries the bother.

idst Stands for 'If Destroyed Still True'. When you carve 'Dan is gay' into his desk and follow it with this abbreviation, even if Dan spends 10 minutes scratching it out it is *still true*.

You can also inscribe INDST so even if it is NOT destroyed it is STILL TRUE.

A second IDST can also protect the first IDST, in case someone destroys the IDST first, rendering the actual message destroyable. But that could result in an endless chain of IDSTs, which would be lunacy.

Girls can develop this into a complex legal system, with further abbreviations like IDEMT (if destroyed even more true), IDEMTTEB and IDSTFEAE – it got to the point where they'd get so caught up in drafting the intricate consequences of the graffiti's destruction that they'd leave out the message altogether.

It is a matter of interpretation as to whether *amending* the graffiti is destroying it. For instance, scratching 'not' in the middle of 'Dan is gay'; although then you might fall foul of the rules in *I'm not gay!*

idunnop The funniest joke of all time. Nothing else even comes close. What you do is, right ... what you do ... whoo! Hang on. Right, OK. You approach the unsuspecting victim with the usual 'Knock, Knock' setup. When they say 'Who's there?', the idiot, you reply... 'IDUNNOP.'

Then the other person has no option but to reply 'I done a poo', and you can laugh for the rest of your life.

if you're happy and you know it There was an emotional conditioning song at school: 'If you're happy and you know it clap your hands.' If you weren't happy (or were happy, but didn't know it), then technically you shouldn't clap, but if you didn't clap you got told off, so you learned to smile and join in and keep the dark thoughts for the bedroom.

If you insist on being a bad citizen and not being happy at all times, then you may change the words 'clap your hands' to 'crap your pants'.

illy dilly dog's willy

Another way of choosing who is 'it', this time based on encouraging an inside-out dog's penis to shit itself by pressing a button.

Illy Dilly Dog's Willy
Inside Out
Press A Little Button
And the shit flies... OUT!

indelible make-up

An involuntary makeover, using a fat-tipped permanent marker. Works better on blonde children.

Draw a Mexican moustache, glasses, sideburns and maybe write 'fuck' on one cheek for good measure. If you go over it a couple of times it will remain visible for days.

If the kid already wears glasses, a variation is to colour in the lens.

indicator mash potato

Something that you shouldn't walk around saying, whilst making windscreen wiper motions with your arms, after the age of nine.

infinity plus one

Where lots of arguments end up.

'You guffed!'
'Yeah well you guffed twice.'
'Yeah well you guffed times a hundred!'
'Yeah well you guffed infinity times!'
'Yeah well you guffed infinity times plus one!'
'You can't have infinity plus one!'
'Yes you can!'
'All right, you guffed infinity times two times!'
'Plus one.'
'Infinity squared!'
'Plus one.'
'Oh fuck off.'

interesting books, how to find

Pages 63 and 64 of the novelisation of *The Terminator* contain a graphic depiction of Sarah Connor's flatmate and her boyfriend having wild sex. When dropped, the book would magically fall open to these pages.

Using this effect: when deciding which library book to take out from the school library, simply hold the book by

interesting books, how to find

Fig One: *The Collins Mini-Gem of British Birds*
This book remains untouched since arriving in
the library during Ornithology Week. The page
featuring the Great Tit might be missing.

Fig Two: *The Fog*, James Herbert
This book contains one well-thumbed scene of
explicit sex and explosive death (*see Fog, The*).
These pages will naturally separate to this passage.

Fig Three: *Women in Love*, DH Lawrence
This book has attracted some interest thanks to
rumours of hot lesbo scissor action. However,
Lawrence's tendency to couch sex in irritating
metaphor makes the passages eminently
unwankable. You will notice a slight fanning
from occasional browsing, though.

Fig Four: *Razzle*
If you find a book like this, it is likely that it had
pictures in it, and all the good ones have been
ripped out. Contrary to popular myth, most people
don't wank directly onto their pornography, so
you won't get pregnant or gay by touching it.

the covers, and turn it upside down. The 'well thumbed' pages, containing either breasts or imaginative death, would fall apart.

More pages grouped together mean more racy passages, which you can then learn and mumble under your breath instead of saying the Lord's Prayer in assembly. *See illustration.*
See also: Fog, The

invisible dog Invisible dogs lived in long school corridors. Because they were invisible, they were prone to getting stepped on by unaware children. They therefore required up to 40 keepers, who lined both sides of the corridor and defended the hound by kicking the shit out of anyone walking through the corridor, and shouting 'Mind the dog!'

A variant on *invisible dog* was *pinball*, where you simply kicked the person without bothering to pretend there was an invisible dog.

ipmat The stages of mitosis are *interphase, prophase, metaphase, anaphase* and *telophase*. To help mem-

orise this meaningless set of words, we were encouraged to think of mnemonics. 'I Porked Michelle's Anal Tract' was ably met with 'I Prefer Masturbation Any Time'. If you'd seen Michelle, you'd have known what the lad meant.

is it 'rape', sir? Offered as an answer to the question, 'If you got mugged on Orpington high street, what should you shout to get help?'

it's my uncle Classic story of that thicko child. Child bunks off school, answers the phone at his house, and when asked, 'Is that you, Ian?', the hypothetical Ian replies, 'No, it's my uncle.' From the same stable of anecdotes as the sicknote that reads, 'Please let my son off games because he has a broken ear. Signed, my mum.'

Very possibly, neither one of these things has ever happened.

it, variations on the theme of
- *run conchita*: like 'it', but you punch

the person in the kidneys and shout 'Run, conchita!'

- *pineapple salesman*: the person who was 'it' was the pineapple salesman, and had to be chased and severely beaten.

- *the bill, the bill, get the bastards*: split into two teams and a pineapple salesman. Each team has a walkie-talkie. The team who gets the pineapple salesman lets the other team listen to the beating on their walkie-talkie.

J j

jabba One of the more punned names in science fiction. Jabba the Hutt was a slovenly, debauched character who ceased his joyless consumption only to watch women dance and murder those who crossed him. Jabba the Mutt was any fat, ugly girl, or those bug-eyed King Charles spaniels who look like they'll explode with even the gentlest application of a woodwork vice to their head. Jabba the Slut applied to any fat girl who shows an interest in sex. Finally, Pizza the Hutt was one of the weaker jokes amongst the many weak jokes in Mel Brooks' *Spaceballs*.

jacobs Product placement version of *soggy biscuit*. The tastelessness and dryness of a Jacob's Cream Cracker, however, made the game even more unpalatable; at least with a Jaffa Cake you'd have a bit of sponge and an orangey bit to hide the taste of willy whites. ***See also: soggy biscuit***

jammy runaround The Keystone Kops-style chases that ensued whenever we decided to force-feed the class diabetic jam doughnuts in the name of research.
See also: peanut shootout

japs and brits

This game involved running around shooting each other with guns. Having no uniforms or other way of distinguishing between the two sides, you had to ask 'Jap or Brit?' before shooting. Luckily, real wars are more organised, with different sides wearing easily distinguishable colours, except for spies, who wear black.

je suis fatigué

'A friend of mine was habitually ridiculed by his French teacher – of all people – over his weight problem and alternative lifestyle. The classroom humiliation took the form of him being asked to say he was tired in French to which he would have to reply, "Je suis fatty-gay." We laughed, the French teacher laughed, the fat child ate another consolatory Battenberg.'

'A moins que' was also a good way of letting stupid people announce to the class that they were wankers.

jelly cubes

Jelly cubes – the kind that your mum dissolved in boiling water to make a Sunday treat – could be moistened with spit to make cheap alternatives to those sticky octopuses that crawl down windows, leaving a pleasing smear.

jesus christ, superstar

Jesus Christ, Superstar
Went round the corner on a Yamaha
Did a skid,
Killed a kid,
Went back to heaven on a dustbin lid.
The idea that Jesus would come to earth, cause death by reckless driving, then return to heaven on a flying dustbin lid, was cheerfully sacrilegious. It doesn't end there, though. Other versions had the last line severing Jesus's bollocks on the dustbin lid – and then continuing along these lines:

When I die, bury me,
Hang up my bollocks on a cherry tree.
When they're ripe, take a bite,
But don't blame me if you fart all night.

When I die, bury me,
Hang my bollocks on a cherry tree.
If they grow, let me know,
Cos I'll be listening on the radio.

The practicalities of grafting human testicles on to a cherry tree – or of gaining valuable radio airtime for an announcement concerning their progress – were not considered, although it is somewhat impressive that in the former version, the lyricist took steps to protect himself against any flatulence-related legal proceedings. This final, less involved, version, however,

Jesus Christ, Superstar,
Wears frilly knickers and a Wonderbra
was more directly and punishably blasphemous, especially if you mimed Jesus looking into a mirror and playing with his own nipples.

jimmy savile

The last person's voice to completely break can be mocked for sounding like Jimmy Savile; forget that two weeks ago the classroom sounded like some demented Savile menagerie.

jinx

'This game is a common one, but for some people the rules need clearing up, because to this day I keep jinxing people and they don't seem to know what I'm talking about, and act all shocked and hurt when I punch them in the arm. It's been on *The Simpsons*, so there's no excuse. So, this is the deal, right?

'If we say the same thing at the same time, then either of us may say 'Jinx'. The jinxed person then cannot speak until anyone – not just the jinxer – says their full name. If they talk before this happens, the jinxer (me) gets to punch the jinxee (you) in the arm. You broke a jinx. You deserve it.

'And another thing, if I ask you a really easy question, then say the answer at the same time, then shout JINX at you, don't say, "Well why did you ask me if you know the answer, and another thing, why did you just shout jinx?" Because if you DO say that, you'll be talking whilst jinxed, and by GOD, I will punch you. (In the arm.)'

jinx, advanced

- *The Jinxee Loophole*: During a jinx, if you can anticipate what your jinxer is about to say, and say it at the same time, this negates the original jinx.

When jinxed, of course, you can't feed questions which might produce predictable results, and if you anticipate incorrectly, you've broken your jinx and you will get punched.

The original jinxer can use this rule to take the piss:

Jinxer: What do you call those people who make bread? Oh, now I remember, and I'm going to say the word after three. 3... 2... 1...

Jinxee: Baker!

Jinxer: No, it was Jeff. Here, have a punch in the arm.

• *'American Jinx (Touch Wood)'*: Instead of declaring a normal jinx, you may shout 'American jinx, touch wood'. The first person to find some wood and touch it may punch the other person on the arm. Normal jinx rules then apply.

jizz Saucy replacement for '*cheers*'.

joey deacon A gift to a generation of children who, previously, had been perfectly happy just laughing at stupid and fat people. Joey Deacon was *Blue Peter*'s attempt to raise awareness and understanding of cerebral palsy. Joey's condition was alarming to children who valued their motor functions and facial expressions, so he was quickly adopted as a figure of ridicule, and the speed at which the word 'spastic' was adopted as an insult led to *The Spastics Society* changing their name (*see scoper*).

Joey's plight was rendered somewhat bizarre by the introduction of other characters. Welcome, please, Ernie Roberts, the only person who could understand Joey's speech. Ernie's condition was less severe, and he would listen to Joey and translate to the presenters of *Blue Peter*. The potential for abuse here was obvious.

Then it got weirder again when Joey started to write a book, *Tongue Tied*. Neither Joey nor Ernie could type. So Michael Sangster and Tom Blackburn were recruited, and the four of them sat around a table, writing Joey's autobiography at the rate of 75 words a day. The idea of the team as separate limbs of a really clunky robot is not terribly respectful, but then neither was getting Simon Groom to say 'How are you today, Joey?' with no intention of listening to his indecipherable response.

Back in the playground, the game of Joey A-Con was born: player one says Joey A-Con, the next player would say Joey B-Con, until the fourth player said 'Joey Deacon', and everyone just starting grunting and falling over. A longer version included Joe-A, Joe-B, Joe-C, Joe-D, Joe-EEEEEE.

johnny halfdick Another name for a circumcised boy, the foreskin being 50% of the weight, volume and joy of the male sexual organ, or winkle. *See also: stinger; b.t.*

john's not mad *John's Not Mad* – a QED documentary of the late 80s. Meet John Davidson, a gentle child from Galashiels, who suffered from a severe case of Tourette's Syndrome. As children recovered from laughing at cerebral palsy, they were given something much more *useful* to play with.

John Davidson simply couldn't stop swearing. As it was educational, none of the swearing was censored. We heard the word 'cunt' coming from the television set, in what amounted to state-sanctioned filth. Swearing, we learned, was acceptable within a certain playfield; and that playfield was Tourette's Syndrome. The next school day saw thousands of children fall ill with a 24-hour version of Tourette's – the only illness that made children *want* to go to school.

This show was released on DVD in 2004, after a follow-up documentary rekindled interest in swearing and screaming children. John Davidson appeared on daytime television to plug it. The same shameless and reprehensible peddling of nostalgia and filth for profit is the fundamental premise behind this book.

jumble-gippo A *Trevor* or *Bronno* who wears the clothes of others. Usually inferred from overt signs of poverty (tousled hair, Blue Riband biscuits), as it was hard to tell from the clothes themselves. Ideally you would find the ultimate evidence – another person's name tag in their clothes. With any luck, it wouldn't be yours, as you might catch the retrospective lurgy.

jumping on animals

It is not true that animals' eyes pop out when you jump on them. Nor is it true that you can inflate frogs by inserting a straw into their anus, because frogs can't belch so there's nowhere for the air to go. Finally, and this one's really upsetting, seagulls *don't* explode when you feed them bread with Alka-Seltzer.

Knowing this will save many children valuable time that would be better spent engineering wars between colonies of red and black ants.

jump the sandy sick

Provided great pleasure for a select few children who enjoyed jumping over sick which had been covered in sand, while a child of more tender sensibilities ran to fetch the caretaker, who was probably the one who had covered it in sand to avoid cleaning it up in the first place.

jungle beats

Two people would grab a smaller boy and pin him to the ground. One would sit on his stomach, whilst the other held his hands. Then there would be a terrible fire in the jungle which was just to the left of the victim, and all the animals would have to escape across the only bridge, which was the victim's chest. First of all came the ants, which were relatively painless. Then the mice and so on, up to the elephants whose heavy feet would cause serious sternum damage.

Among the best escapees were the lions and tigers with their sharp claws, and the kamikaze butterflies, who would hover for a while before crashing with unjustifiable force. Also very painful were the electric nipple-cripple ants who only came along in extended versions of *Jungle Beats*.

just because you've got hair around your lips doesn't mean you have to talk like a cunt

When said to a bearded teacher, will result in at least one detention. Come to think of it, you'd probably get a detention from a teacher without a beard, although they would probably look a little more confused.

K K

Kapraaa The jubilant sound one should make when launching handfuls of foam ripped from the bus seats out of the back window, and on to the windscreen of the jeep behind, causing it to swerve wildly.

Keyboards, electronic, the demonstration tunes of When the electronic keyboards were brought out, there would be a rush to press *Demonstration Tune: Start/Stop*. These showcase tunes would demonstrate every voice on the keyboard in a magnificent rendition of the *Star Trek* theme, or *Air on a*

G-String. When 'Axel F' (the theme from *Beverly Hills Cop*) was included as the demonstration tune, it caused many children to throw themselves against the wall or to the floor and scream 'Get the fuck outta here!' like a real cop played by Eddie Murphy would.

Kick the martin Martin would be asked a question. If he answered it correctly he was kicked once. If he answered incorrectly he was kicked twice. If he didn't answer at all he was kicked until he did. Best questions therefore were along the lines of '*Do you shag dogs?*' or '*Do you fancy old* men?' where the only way to minimise the abuse was to give the 'correct' answer of Yes.

KICKSIES A variant of football in which the pursuit of goals was scorned in favour of 'nutmegging'* the weakest child, who would then become the Gaylord, and be attacked until he could touch the oak tree, which stopped him being gay.

Kiddy in the middle A game devised to administer as much pain as possible on one person.

The Kiddy In The Middle is nominated by any accepted method: birthday, new shoes, anyone who answered too many questions in class, first person to get pointed at. The Kiddy In The Middle then lies down, and attempts to stand up whilst everyone else kicks him back down. There was only one unspoken rule – that you did not kick the face; this rule was adhered to

because you knew that your time in the middle would inevitably come.

This may sound brutal, but in one school it had a heart-warming conclusion:

'When it came to the school bully's birthday, the largest crowd assembled for the ritual game of Kiddy In The Middle. The bully could see that he was going to get the kicking of his lifetime but he couldn't back out, as he was the main instigator of the game. Normal Kiddy etiquette, however, was out of the window; there were too many old scores to settle.

'He got his kicking; and it was wonderful to see those long-bullied victims taking their revenge, safe in the knowledge that their legs would be lost in a blur of other legs and blood. It was the rare moment of resolution that you only normally see on television. A perfect day.'

Kids' Army An invented army that compulsively lying children may join

---

* You are 'nutmegged' when the ball passes between your legs. Usually an accidental practice, enforced nutmegging can require two people to hold the victim's legs as far apart as possible.

It's like the real army, but they let kids in. But you have to be really tough, and they give you real guns and bullets. Should any child in the kids' army get invited to a real-life event on a day when he would normally be out shooting enemies, he may quickly say, 'It's OK, I shot my sergeant with a sub-machine gun last week so they said I could have this week off.'

Kind or mean?

A game where you ask an unassuming, quiet child whether he is kind or mean, then ignore his answers, only to repeat the question in a more complex variation.

A: Are you kind or are you mean?

B: Leave me alone.

A: Because if you're mean you can't be kind, and if you're kind you can't be mean, which means you're kind of mean, or are you mean of kind?

B: Shut up.

A: MEAN CHILD!

B: Go away.

A: KIND BOY!

Continue until the child becomes reduced to tears.

King Cnut

Graffiti daubed on the school wall, circa 1980 :

Whoever said punk's dead is a Cnut

'At least that's what I thought it said. Eight years old and convinced that it was a grave insult to compare someone to the viking king of England (1016–1035). I tried to explain to my peers that Cnut had been a good king; that the popular myth of him trying to turn back the sea was wrong, and thus this was not a very effective insult. It was about that time that the beatings began.'

King of the table

'The title bestowed to the first person back to their table after lunch break. There was no crown, and the King of the Table's sole power was to be allowed to sharpen the communal crayons on the teacher's special windy-handled desk-mounted sharpener.

'Wayne Hales would generally win, not through athleticism, but through brute force. He would swing and maul his way to the title, then set about daintily sharpening crayons for us for the rest of the lesson.'

Kippering 'A game in which you asked a friend a question to which you already knew the answer.

'At the game's most base level, for example, you may ask "Is this a banana?" while clearly holding a banana in front of the proposed kippering victim. If he replied with a straight answer to the question then he had been "kippered", and the correct response of the kipperer was to adopt a dramatically pained expression and look away while exhaling heavily, usually following up with the phrase, "Ooh, kippered him a treat." If the proposed victim spotted the kipper coming, saying "You're all right, mate" would block it.

'The game died a natural death after a couple of months when no conversation could occur among my friends without a dozen kippering attempts and everyone was constantly on their guard to the point of replying to any spoken word with "You're all right, mate".'

Kiss chase Running around, imagining that you know what an erection is, and hoping to touch a girl's gusset peach. Had you managed it, you would have been sick. As these two stories show, *kiss chase* allowed for some of the earliest expressions of 'girl power'.

'Kiss chase could also be extremely dangerous. I, for one, broke my arm chasing a weedy little boy. Damn, I wanted that kiss.'

'When I was invited to join the Kissing Girls – the exclusive club for the most popular girls in the school – I was naturally very excited. The sole purpose of the club was to chase boys around and kiss anyone they caught, amidst vague protestations of "ick". One day, I chased down a boy, rugby-tackled him to the ground, and then, when he refused to hold still, I jabbed him in the face with a sharp stick. I wasn't able to kiss him, because he was too busy crying and holding his bleeding face in his hands while everyone else looked on, aghast.

'I suspect that it was my failure to deliver the kiss that was the reason the Kissing Girls never let me play with them again.'

KUDOS K

KiSS flaps The flap of material in the back of your blazer, right next to your arse. The 'kiss flap' was used by homosexual men when they wanted to do something to your bottom, whatever it is that gay men do to bottoms. Probably kiss them, if the name *kiss flaps* is anything to go by.

KnOck KnOck jOkeS Joke that you can use on the children of Jehovah's Witnesses.

> *Knock knock.*
> *Who's there?*
> *It's your mum and dad.*

See also: idunnop (which is the funniest joke in the world. Seriously, you'll love it)

KOnStant cUmmin9 A book, entitled *Beginnings*, was co-written by John Cumming and David Konstant. David had clearly contributed more to the book, so his name had to feature first on the spine of the book.

Therefore, this read KONSTANT/CUMMING: BEGINNINGS, which made it seem like the first instalment of the spunkiest saga in the world.

The book was, in fact, about Christianity.

KUdOS Completely random careers advising computer program, along with Cascaid. Both programs were loaded with the most obscure professions, advising previously well-adjusted children to become morgue attendants and book-binders. Alarmingly often, however, children were advised to become wig-makers.

According to these programs, so many people would make great wig-makers, it's surprising that there aren't more wigs in the world. Perhaps there are ... if everyone turned out to be really good wigmakers, no one would realise that everyone was bald.

God, is everyone bald?
See illustration overleaf.

KUDOS

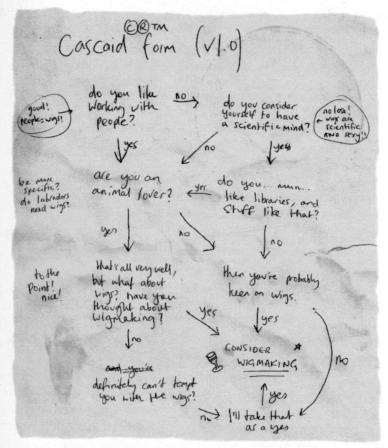

Cascaid ©®™ form (v1.0)

good! people = wigs!

do you like working with people? — no → do you consider yourself to have a scientific mind?

no lose! ← wigs are scientific AND sexy!!

↓ yes

no

↓ yes

be more specific? do labradors need wigs?

are you an animal lover? ← yes — do you... mmm... like libraries, and stuff like that?

↓ yes

no

↓ no

to the point! nice!

That's all very well, but what about wigs? have you thought about wigmaking?

then you're probably keen on wigs.

yes

↓ yes

↓ no

CONSIDER WIGMAKING

no

~~and you're~~ definitely can't tempt you with the wigs?

↑ yes

no → I'll take that as a yes ←

The logic behind the Cascaid form, before pressure from non-wigmaking industries forced them to include **morgue attendant** and **freight handler**, with questions such as "Corpses – Cool or Icky?" and "Pictured opposite is some freight. Do you kinda want to handle it?"

L l

lab assistants Lab assistants, also known as lab technicians, had no real contact with the children. They existed in rooms next to the laboratories, guarding the caesium (highly reactive with water, you see), and occasionally peered through the strip of window on the door that wasn't covered with posters about how interesting science was. These docile heroes populated a limbo, living between classrooms, neither pupil nor teacher.

They had chosen this semi-life surrounded by magnesium, bimetallic strips, and pornography stored on 5.25' floppy disks. This life of putting out test-tube racks and heatproof mats, then hiding before the children arrived.

No one ever saw lab assistants arrive at or leave school.

laboratory, weaponry of the

- **Magnesium ribbon** – a favourite. Produces an intense white light when lit. Can cause temporary blindness if let off in someone's face.

- **Sodium** – produces unimpressive fizzing display when dropped in a sink full of water unless you've got enough to simulate Krakatoa.

Dunking a head in the fizz will cause extreme panic and some flailing.

- **Phosphorus** – the heavyweight. Ignites on contact with the air! Imagine sticking it down someone's collar!

Master these three and you may move on to **caesium**, if you can get the key to the special cupboard.

Another battle-tested chem-lab weapon is a DIY cattle-brand made by heating up a set of test-tube tongs until they are glowing. Then, press them firmly down on a classmate's book, pencil case, tie, blazer, etc., leaving a livid black imprint. Not skin, though. That might *hurt*, and leave a *really cool scar*.

ladybird lorry driving

Bending a ladybird book in the middle, and using it as a steering wheel whilst 'driving' along the lines of the netball pitch. Intelligent children would laugh at the kids who didn't straighten up the book properly after a corner. I mean, if you really were driving a Ladybird Lorry, you'd be going around in circles! You *damned idiots*.

ladybirds, trumping

An overheard story of love and betrayal, shared by a young boy with his friend.

'There is a ladybird on my hand,' said one child to another, on the top deck of a Nottingham bus. 'Oh look, so there is!' replied his friend. A troubled look flicked across the first child's face. 'Yes, but when I stroked it, it trumped on me.'

lambeth walk

We play the Lambeth way,
Not like you but a bit more gay
And we have a bit of fun – oh, boy!

This song makes everyone in the class shout the word gay at the same time. As an additional bonus, the lyrics were written by Noel Gay. This must make 'The Lambeth Walk' the gayest song of all time. Even the Village People never had the balls to use the gay-word.

land crab

Live role-playing is the phenomenon that occurs when those masters of Dungeons & Dragons feel the need to take it out of the living room, and into the local woods. For those children with parents willing to indulge their woeful habit, a day out wielding foam-wrapped wooden swords was their reward.

For those dedicated children whose parents were unwilling to play, the option was to volunteer to be a monster. And one of these monsters was the humble *land crab*. Forced to hide in damp caves for an hour until the 'adventurers' arrived, and then restricted to a naff sideways movement and a threatening clack of the pincers (hands), *land crabs* were pure cannon fodder. The victims of the victims.

Sensing the first physical victory of their lives, these brave adventurers would be merciless; all *land crabs* would be *obliterated*.

language, why latin should remain a dead

'Such was one Latin teacher's love of classical civilisation, he used his pupils as players in an attempt to recreate Ancient Rome in his class. We dressed up in togas (using the long red velvet classroom curtains), and then were asked to "recline like a Roman".

'The pure hedonism of a teacher dressing up his pupils and having them recline on a desk for his approval (yes, that is how a Roman might recline) would eventually prove too flavoursome for modern, non-Roman society.'

la plante magique

A comic strip and cassette-based story in some pre-GCSE French textbooks. Also the act of throwing soil, grass and flowers at someone. The 'magic' is descriptive of the incredible way these missiles mysteriously 'flew' at your head.

laser eyes

The glare that a teacher would give you after any wrongdoing too minor to warrant a verbal ticking off. When receiving *laser eyes*, pupils can protect themselves by holding a protractor or shatterproof ruler over the eyes – refracting the glare into a harmless rainbow of disapproval.

last to sit down

A very simple game – the last person to sit down after entering the classroom wins. Despite the simplicity, the lengths the last two players would go to to avoid sitting down was incredible.

This game generally ends with two people hovering above their chairs and staring at each other, trying to work out from the height of their head whether their arse was – so to speak – touching wood.

laughter, inappropriate

Laughter is inappropriate both when you are told that your geography teacher is dead, and also when a bully comes into class in tears because her heroin-addicted aunt had become a cabbage and had her life support turned off. Inappropriate, but queerly irresistible.

leccy gibbo

'The name of a local Superhero. He gained his powers in a traditionally comic-book way: climbing an electricity pylon from simple scientific curiosity, Gibbo was catapulted 50 feet when the shock inevitably came. He miraculously survived – thus proving his immortality – and when he came to, he found that his IQ had been safely relegated to Sunday Stegosaurus League. Thus was born Leccy Gibbo, the Superhero least likely to ever complete the Rubik's Cube.'

leprosy

After Tourette's Syndrome and Irritable Bowel Syndrome, leprosy is the disease with the funniest symptoms. The idea of things just dropping off generally leads to pupils pleading for more particular details.

What, things drop off? What, like noses? How do noses drop off? Do they slide off? Do you have to pull the last bit off yourself? And fingers, they'd come off ... but what about arms? Can't you hold the arm on with your other arm, or would that arm drop off too? If the arms fell off first, would the fingers fall off later?

No teacher has ever explained leprosy to the entire satisfaction of his or her class.

let's-be-friends

The female equivalent of bum chums, sounding as it does a bit like lesbians. Extended in this rehearsed exchange:

A: Lezbie friends.
B: Homo you don't!
A: Durexpect me to believe that?
B: I'm not in the nude for it!
A: Oh gay then.
B: I breast my case.

let's go! Simpler children generally responded well to encouragement. Simply chanting *'Let's go!'* created such an air of fun-loving approval, that some lesser-gifted children would run around the playing field until they got dizzy and fell over, hyperventilating with joy.

This can't *technically* be termed bullying, because at the end of the day, everyone was happy.

litigation, playground If you were a member of a Suing Club, you could threaten to sue someone if they did something you didn't like. Before a more complete understanding of the civil legal process was gained, it was understood that successfully being sued meant that your parents are taken away, their house removed, the plaintiff gained custody of all toys and the defendant would be forced to live in a cardboard box and eat poo for ever and ever.

little reindeer *'I don't want to see any litter round 'ere.'*

'A basic but sincere misunderstanding of dialect that led to the common belief that our janitor was insane.'

livin' in a box, livin' in a cardboard box *Living In A Box*'s eponymous hit. Proved to be a useful song for when words like gippo and fleabag lost their effect. Could be used in conjunction with 'Uptown Slag, she's been living in a paper bag', by Billy Joel.

lobster An unwelcome erection in the changing rooms. An erection in this situation was treated with the same level of confusion, fear and disgust as if a lobster had, indeed, walked into the changing rooms with a towel wrapped around its waist, and started whistling.

log 'The name for a child so fat and ungainly that when he falls over, a quick-witted bully has the presence of mind to shout "timber", then pretend that the ground shook.

'Technically an insult, should you carry the name into adulthood, you'll be surprised how many people assume you have a gigantic cock. Or do massive poos, which is just as cool to some people. Thanks, that bully!'

logger A chocolate bar which appeared briefly in the mid-80s. Clearly intended to be a butch bar for big boys, the lumberjack masculinity was undermined by the fact that it looked like a shit. And with the name 'Chocolate Logger', it's impossible to pretend that this bar passed through board meetings with no sniggering.

Only more disconcerting than seeing someone scoff a *Logger* and getting chocolate all around their mouth was the Fruit and Nut version; quite frankly, only just short of a Sweetcorn Logger in terms of unappetising confectionery. **See also: big bender in a bun**

look! When a conversation reaches a natural break, suddenly exclaim 'Look!' while pointing enthusiastically. They will naturally turn to look without actually listening to what you're pointing out. Then you get to say what it was you were pointing at. Typical examples include 'Look! An arse!' or the slightly cleverer 'Look! My finger!'

look, the filing cabinet's giving birth – do you like me? A baffling tale of love in a confusing world.

'I was 12, she was in her 30s. She taught R.E., and we were in a storeroom alone together collecting textbooks. And it wasn't me that said it. So much for a Catholic upbringing.'

lost property The Lost Property Offices of some schools are manned at such irregular and unpredictable hours that a good alternative to throwing someone's belongings on to the roof of the bus shelter is simply to hand them in to Lost Property.

It would then be much, much harder

for the owner to reclaim his belongings from Lost Property than from a more conventional hiding place, e.g. the top of a bus shelter (next to the single *Green Flash* trainer) or the Longford River.

love letters

Simply put, just don't write love letters. And don't write love poetry. Ever. But especially not as a child. It's simply revolting and precocious. Even as an adult, the only kind of people you'll attract with the kind of poetry *you're* capable of writing will be vapid bunny-boilers. Love letters. Poetry. Avoid.

The only exception is the love letter 'Can I see your tits', or the poem 'Don't be mean, miss − suck my peenis'. These are OK.

love percentages, calculation of

A simple mathematical method of measuring human attraction, simpler and cheaper than Internet dating profiles. Simply: **1.** Take the names; in this instance we will use Matthew Fasham and Kylie Minogue. **2.** Count the number of occurrences of the letters L, O, V, E and S. Write them down. In this case, 1 − 1 − 0 − 3 − 1. **3.** Add up adjacent numbers to 2 − 1 − 3 − 4. **4.** Again, to get 3 − 4 − 7, then again to 7 − 11.

At this stage, you can either add 7 to 11, to make a heartbreaking 18%, or split the 11 into two 1s, which would result in a love factor of 82% − which would nearly guarantee sex, should Matthew and Kylie meet.

Here is one of the rare, rare times when being an absolute maths nerd can garner you some kudos, with a series of 'amazing' 99% results. First, work out the magical 99% results. One such number* is 12021. Then, take the person's name you wish to matchmake. Say, for example, Matthew Fasham. This scores 00011, so we require 12010 to make it up to 12021.

Then, extend the game to include not only people, but *hobbies* that Matthew Fasham might love.

---

* 01202, 03006, 20210, 31105, 32007, 50113, 51015, 60030, 60106, 80016, and 90009 are others. Interestingly enough.

Thus, we can now surmise that Matthew Fasham loves Felching Poo with every fibre of his soul. Well, 99%, anyway.

lucozade The unfortunate act, whilst *vertical distance pissing*, of over-estimating the best penis angle, resulting in a shower of piss coming down on your own head. The most admired practitioners of *v.d.p.* would gain respect by pushing the envelope and coming dangerously close to a *Lucozade* but still managing to win the competition with dry hair.

See also: distance pissing, vertical

lunchbox hierarchy The elements of a lunchbox are all subject to a scoring system that any child can appraise in seconds. As adults, we may need help with a table.

Your score, coupled with your social standing, will determine your treatment. For instance, a score of 12 is recommended for victims; any noticeable variance from the absolute average will result in unwelcome attention. For popular children, the higher the score the better. In a geek-friendly environment, fruit may actually be considered acceptable. To be honest, it's a more complicated issue than we have room to deal with here.

Just remember: cling film is not an acceptable substitute for a lunch box.

Or, remember, a contraceptive.

Sandwich	Crisps	Snack	Drink
5 Deep filled, fresh, with two or more meats on wholegrain thick sliced bread	Rippled or otherwise textured luxury snack	Proper chocolate bar: Mars, Twix	Can Coke or equivalent
4 Real, unprocessed meats on Mighty White.	Monster Munch or other highly flavoured crisp	Mid-range chocolate: Penguin	Carton Ribena
3 Standard cheese or processed ham on standard white bread.	Ready Salted Walkers	Budget chocolate: Ace, Taxi, Blue Riband	Pouch Capri Sun
2 Elements of sweatiness. Sandwich droops when held by the edge.	10p Red Mill snack – Tangy Toms	Fun-size chocolate	Tupperware beaker Robinson's cordial/ Panda Pops
1 One Kraft Single between two unbuttered slices of a 7p loaf.	None	Two custard creams in cling film. Fruit.	Tap water

M m

mag Shouted and accompanied by a flexing of a little finger. Denotes the possession of a less than impressive member. An abbreviation of maggot, which little willies look like. Variations include, *maggee*, *Mr Magoo*, *magga magga magga* and *magwaaaaah*, this last example shouted in a Zippy-from-*Rainbow* style voice.

The only reversal is, sadly, inelegant. Simply shout back, 'No, you're the MAG! I'm a MONSTER!' Meaning, obviously, that your penis is huge, and very hairy indeed.

'Have you ever seen a maggot spit?'

'No ...'

'Well, wank harder then.'

magical anus smell The smell of the human anus can pass through the fabric of the underpant and trouser. You might have to get your finger right up there, and worm it around for a while, and you're risking severe skidders, but it's worth it if you manage to make someone else smell your finger.

For less effort, but with the risk of Shirley Bassey's Brownfinger, put your hand *inside* your underwear.

magic e A song performed by an animated wizard, who had special e-mazing powers. Voiced by Derek Griffiths, he would sing:

Fat becomes fate with me!
Rat becomes rate with me!
I'm magic, magic Ɛ!

After comically noting that shit becomes shite with him, children would rack their brains, thinking of another rude word ending in a removable 'e'. Thus, pub became pube with e.

And in a cautionary tale for the hip-hop generation, rap becomes rape with E.

magic potion The *magic potion* would be made from a half-empty yoghurt pot, plus added ingredients such as barbecue crisps, bread crusts, apple pips and *anything else to hand*. The challenge was to make it as big and filthy a mix as possible, and for it to be stirred clockwise with the dinner lady's pen, otherwise it wouldn't work.

The hapless yoghurt owner would then have to eat this mess. If successful and they were able to keep the mix down for more than 10 minutes, they were crowned 'the Great Sage' for the lunchtime. If they lost the contents of lunch within the 10 minutes, they were made to eat grass, because that's what cats do when they have a dodgy stomach.

mamma mia Pleasingly close to diarrhoea. 'Mamma Mia / I've got diarrhoea / Plip-Plop / Can you hear my shit drop?' is a good example of this similarity in action.

manners! Inverted reproach for lack of courtesy in oneself. Simply ask a favour, without saying please. If the subject complies, you may shout 'MANNERS!' at the top of your voice, and reject their offer. That'll teach them for being nice to rude people like you.

man train The pleasurable experience of pressing your buttocks into another boy's crotch, and bouncing up and down a bit, combined with the pleasurable experience of having another boy press his buttocks into your groin and bouncing up and down a bit. Repeat until you run out of boys. No girls are allowed.

This is in no way homosexual, homoerotic, or anything other than lots of straight boys having an innocent non-sexual bumming session.

martial arts

Do not admit to learning any martial art, unless you are quite prepared, and physically able, to follow it up.

'The smallest kid in our year, sick of being the victim, screamed "I've learned Tae-Kwon Do" as a half-hearted bullying session began. To astonished looks from his assailants, he proceeded to strike a number of ridiculous Bruce Lee-style poses, while going an unhealthy shade of red. His mastery of the ancient Korean martial art was such that the first punch laid him out, whereupon the bullying resumed. Only now it wasn't quite so half-hearted.'

mash and bean pants

'The slow kid was often asked to do something which he believed would make him popular. The most enjoyable requests were for him to fill his underpants up with mashed potato or baked beans and go and show the teachers.'

mashed potatoes?

A dinner-queue offer, best riposted with the hilarious, *'No, it's just the way my trousers hang.'*

Also applicable to offers of boiled sprouts, grated carrot, hot plums, twisted bacon and erect sweetcorn.

metalwork

The only lesson in which it is possible to make death stars, and burn the ceiling with welding equipment.

mighty mouse is on the way

*Mighty Mouse is on the way.
Here he comes to make
your day even greener.*

Sing this to your friends, then pretend to bring up bogies. It doesn't scan like the original song, and relies on the phrase, 'I'm having a bit of a green day,' which doesn't even exist. Shit.

millionaires you know, tramps who are really

To alleviate the guilt that comes from a lifestyle of comparative luxury, a universal lie told to children is that *tramps are really millionaires, you know*. This transforms the tragedy of poverty and mental illness into a Buddhist lifestyle choice.

The main reasons given by parents for this decision is that he woke up one day and realised that *money can't bring you happiness*. This also explained why you couldn't have the Millennium Falcon, and had to make do with a shitty Stormtrooper, who wasn't even an Imperial Stormtrooper.

mini kievs Hands-on parody of the popular TV advert in which a mother would shout *'mini kievs!'* and her family would drop everything and rush to the dining table.

A classmate would poke his head round the door just as a lesson was about to start. He or she would shout *'mini kievs!'*, and the entire class would run cheerfully out of the lesson. Never to return.

minter A child with an exceptionally small penis. i.e. a penis so small, it could fit in the hole of a Polo mint.

Accusations of *minterdom* are often not even backed up with evidence gained from a sighting. But then, you'd have to be gay to be looking at cocks anyway, so that's OK. ***See also: mag***

mirror, mirror, can't say it back 'Mirror, mirror, can't say it back, no returns, butcher rules.' Said after an insult, to insulate you from retorts. With any luck, the other person won't even remember what the insult was by the time you've finished preventing them from replying.

miss When playing Battleships in study period, under the tolerant eye of a female teacher, be sure to report unlucky guesses with a plaintive 'Miss ...', thus ensuring that she constantly has to look up from her work.

miss holland 'If you're Miss Holland, there must be some fucking ugly people in Holland.'

missile swindle, the great swizzle According to a

more hysterical teacher, if dropped from the tower block windows, Swizzle lollies would *act like a missile*, and if a child looked up and was hit by such a lolly, *the contents of his eye would literally spill out!*

Naturally, young imaginations were set alight, and many experiments ensued with kids being forced to look up with open eyes at the windows while lollies were aimed at their face. The results were disappointing and spill-free.

mo Abbreviation of 'homo'. Gay. The shortest word for gay there is.

Mo & Mo had a porno store,
Bumming each other behind the door.
See also: molybdenum

molybdenum In the periodic table, the element molybdenum (atomic weight 42) has the abbreviation of 'Mo'. Short for homo, anyone scoring 42% on any exam would be unable to argue that they are anything other than a 100% vagina-decliner.

mong Mong no longer means exclusively 'child affected by Down's Syndrome', but now includes:

Children tripping over, children failing to answer a question, children who can't climb over the wall all their mates just climbed over, children who take more than seven seconds to tie their shoelaces, children who stutter, children who wear glasses, and children with DNA.

Everyone is a mong at some point in their life.

monks, uncommon misconceptions regarding
Monks in France, right, they used to suck mercury off the floor using their anuses, hold it in their rectums for short amounts of time, then let it back out again. Doing this aided relaxation and provided relief from stress.

Although this turned out to be untrue, a *genuinely real* book by Hiroyuki Nishigaki called *How to Goodbye Depression: If You Clench Anus A Hundred Times Every Day. Malarkey? or Effective Way?* offers a similar philosophy, only with less of the sucking mercury up it.

MS. In the time pre-post-feminism, this was the title of choice for some female teachers who refused to be identified on the basis of their marital status.

Roughly translated, *too old to be single, too dowdy to be married*. Whispered accusations of lesbianism would follow.

muffs, pissing into The mistaken belief that sexual intercourse necessarily involved urinating into a girl's vagina. Vaginas should be referred to as *muffs*. Using the word vagina outside of a *genital interrogation* probably meant that you were a girl or a gaymobender.

As a sexual practice, feel free to call this a 'golden egg yolk'.

mum What not to call the chemistry teacher in class, or any other time for that matter.

Unless, by some strange quirk of fate she is your mum, but that's such a diseased idea that it would make you her uncle or something.

music and movement In the days before multimedia, there was BBC Schools Radio. 'Music And Movement' was their public service to avoid PE teachers going into meltdown under the strain of ever having to have a single idea, ever. Soothingly-voiced routines of well-to-do men and women saying 'I'm a tree, I'm a tree, be a tree with me'. If it wasn't real life, this would have been a *Sapphire & Steel* plotline in which hypnotised tree-children attempted to set down their roots in the ground where a soldier once died.

music room, weaponry of the

- *The Glockenspiel Beater*: This weapon could be thrown with pinpoint accuracy to contact with a desired part of a victim's anatomy with almost no effort. It is one of the subtler weapons as it can easily be launched by a nonchalant flick of the wrist whilst the assailant casually stares in the other direction. Beater throwing is best fun if the head of the beater can be removed and thrown independently from the stick, thus giving a two-fold attack strategy.

- *The Coconut Shells*: These are for your more tactical assailant. They can either be used for the basic 'trap someone's fingers in them as they slap shut at 47 mph' gag OR, for the slightly more adventurous attacker, put one coconut shell over some unsuspecting victim's ear and hit with a beater (see above) until victim has a perforated ear-drum.
- *The Xylophone Keys*: Hard, wooden, heavy, sharp. So many possibilities, so little time.
- *The Snare Drum Brush*: Most popular of all. This tightly bound weapon, consisting of half horse-hair and half wire, is most effective when drawn agonisingly slowly over naked flesh – popular with the 'fat kid' bully network.
- *Maracas*: The hand-grenades of the music room arsenal. Best launched from the upper platform in the drama studio, maracas would explode on contact with floor or head, scattering the enemy with small white pellets and imaginary gobbets of flaming napalm.
- *Sheet music*: 'Although not a regular weapon, at our school a boy was sent to hospital after the kid who was handing out sheet music decided to just throw it at the class, and cut the boy's eyeball open.' (Possibly not true.)

muu, by dabe's ... A proper response to a stupid comment. During the insult, the tongue of the insulter is pressed into the gap between the bottom lip and the teeth. An example:

A: *What does 'wank' mean?*
B: *Muu, my name's B, and I'm a spack.*
A: *But ... hang on, I'm A. You're B.*
B: *Yeah, I got it wrong.*
A: *Spack.*
See also: errhhhuuuuu!; gay

my aunt nellie

My Aunt Nellie had a hole in her belly
And a hole in the biscuit tin.

She was sitting on the grass
With her finger up her arse
And her tits going ding-a-ling-a-ling.
Another song may explain what the biscuit tin was for:

Olly olly olly,
Put your tits in the trolley,
and your balls in the biscuit tin.
So, the hole was possibly to allow the balls to breathe.

my friend billy had a ten-foot willy

The definitive version of this hardy perennial primary-school classic follows:

My friend Billy had a 10-foot willy,
He showed it to the girl next door.
She thought it was a snake
So she hit it with a rake
And now it's only 2 foot 4.

In some areas, the willy was left at a rather more impressive 5 foot 4, which would have been of some small consolation to Billy, who would have suffered considerable rake trauma and the loss of his helmet.

my little pony

The first line is uncontroversial:

My little pony, skinny and bony.
After which, you have options: *Under the table, drinking Black Label; Made out of plastic, looks like a spastic; Looked in the mirror, and saw a Godzilla* (whether My Little Pony had a Godzilla behind her, or chronic self-image problems, we cannot say); *Went to the circus, and done it on purpose* ('it' being a poo, probably).

N n

naffco54 The range of cheap Saturday market coats as worn by poor children. Inspired the song 'Nanny Annie Fishy Fanny Condom Fifty-Four'.

Meanwhile, in Pikeyville, owning a NaffCo54 jacket was the 'supa-biznitch'. People in real Naf Naf coats were pointed and laughed at for being a bunch of hoity-toity poofs. It's a matter of perspective, really.

naked fuzzy felt life of jesus A sacrilegious abuse of quasi-adhesive fabric.

'We were told a bizarre story from the Bible about Jesus arriving at a city and the children being so happy that they took off all their clothes, and threw them at him. The idea of people taking their clothes off is more than any group of six-year-olds should be expected to deal with, but this dirty, dirty story was illustrated with Fuzzy Felt.

'Never have so many children been so shocked by an utter lack of anything shocking.'

nan flaps The swinging flap of chunkmeat that hangs from dinner ladies' upper arms. Also known as *bingo wings*.

nature girls, the

A group of about six girls, who claimed to be an 'environmental' group and as such received permission to use the library for 'meetings'. There was even a logo, drawn on official membership cards and note-books (crafted from stapled foolscap).

'The name of the club was simply a cover for its real purpose, which was to sit around and write secret-code gossipy messages about Andrea. The club lasted for a week, until the rest of the class found out about *the Nature Girls* and its crappy name and laughed it out of existence. Andrea amongst them, the bitch.'

nazi chair arrangements

'The swastika is a potent symbol. It evokes the atrocities of the 1940s more than any other. So when you make one out of chairs in a school where three out of ten pupils are Jewish, you can expect the teachers, parents, and even some non-Jewish pupils to take a dim view of it.

'What did we learn from our adventures? That extreme right-wing politics, fascism and genocide are *bad things*.'

nearly knickers

A cruel show performed by girls, built on the relentless requests by boys for a flash of their knickers. The skirt would be lifted and folded in a carefully calculated fan-formation to the following song:

One, two, three, four,
Come on boys and see some more!
Five, six, seven, eight,
Sorry boys you're just too late.

At this point the skirt would be released back to its full length, just before any part of the knickers had been revealed, leaving the boys to punch their own palms in cartoonish frustration.

new, are you?

A question for upper sixth formers to ask first years.

'Hello, are you new?' The first year would invariably think they were extending the hand of friendship and answer 'Yes'. At this point the sixth former would say 'Hello New' and he and all his friends would collapse with laughter.

After a few times, when you had wised up, you might try replying 'No'.

This was met with the logically baffling 'Hello, No' and laughter which was slightly louder, in case you tried to point out the flaws in the response.

nicholas Sounds a bit like knicker-less. Even combined with Parsons, this still isn't really very funny. Sorry, it's just not.

nipple gripple A playful, yet painful, pinch and twist motion on the nipple, *aka* nipple cripple, tit-nip. At a certain stage in your physical development, you might suddenly begin to find this pleasurable, and start looking dreamily at bulldog clips.
See also: purple nurple

nipple patrol An extension of the *nipple gripple* that often got out of hand. On a quiet and rainy lunchtime one boy would *nipple gripple* another boy until they gave up and agreed to join the patrol. They would then go and find another boy and *nipple gripple* him until he also 'joined the patrol'. This would go on until there was a stupidly

large group of boys, and new boys were becoming increasingly difficult to find. (Apart from the boy eating his lunch alone, and looking dreamily at a bulldog clip.)

Girls were obviously taboo, because it was thought that the nipples might come off, and bottles of milk would fall out.

nits Ignore reassurances that '*nits only live in really clean hair*'. The nurse only told you that to make you feel better. In reality, you revolted even the nurse, who'd seen bone sticking out of legs and *everything*.

nob-chicken The act of getting your cock out, and keeping it out as long as possible before public sympathy wanes, your bottle goes, or a teacher sees you and their tongue drops out like a carpet.

noddy and big ears, big thrills for Perfect for situations where your friends were bragging about their new birthday/

Christmas presents. '*Oooo*,' you'd reply. '*Big thrills for Noddy and Big Ears.*'

Clearly, Noddy and Big Ears were notoriously easy to thrill.

norfolk punch An attack where you punch your victim from both sides, in either kidney. Also known in one school as a B-52, or a Rock Lobster.

normans After playing *speednob* on your exercise book, one method of disguise is making them look like Norman soldiers. This is done by extending the 'jap line' down beyond the 'head line', making the nose guard of the helmet, and adding a face. Additional realism could be achieved by adding a little arm holding a spear, or sword, and shield.

See the illustrations overleaf for some alternative penis cover-ups.

See also: speednob

nose limits At a time when the 2unlimited shit classic 'No Limits' was riding high in the charts, this became a brief insult for the bigger-nosed members of the school:

> *Nose Nose, Nose-Nose*
> *Nose Nose, Nose-Nose*
> *Nose Nose, Your Nose*
> KNOWS NO LIMITS
> *It knows no limits – it reaches the sky,*
> *it flies round the room –*
> *and pokes out my eye.*

no shit, sherlock A fair-enough thing to say in response to an observation of the obvious.

The smarmy reply of 'Keep shovelling, Watson' should never be used. Talking like The Two Ronnies should be limited *exclusively* to talking about naughty sketches like 'The Phantom Raspberry Blower of Old London Town'.

nothing A craze that went on for far too long was urgently catching someone's attention, then saying 'oh, nothing' as though they were cretins for asking. The more effort that went into gaining the person's attention, the more satisfying the *nothing*.

Another variant is the slightly more

sophisticated and therefore insufferable 'Can I just interrupt you there?' and when they reply 'Yes' you say 'Thanks', and walk off.

n't The most economical way to contradict someone who was accusing you of something. In use:

A: *Your trainers are from Jonathan James.*

B: *No they aren't.*

A: *Yes they are.*

B: *N't.*

A: *Are.*

B: *N't.*

Repeat to fade, or until either party starts using multipliers or infinity. In which case, see *infinity plus one*.

nuclear hand grenades An offshoot of the arms race of the Cold War. Nuclear hand grenades worked like regular hand grenades, only you were given a few seconds longer to run away from the two-mile radius of absolute destruction, and hide underneath a mattress.

nutjob Someone of lower intelligence than the rest of their group. Nutjobs were often administered *chapatees*, swift slaps to the forehead that made such a satisfying noise that people would turn from their conversations to say, 'Man, that's good chapatee.'

Normans

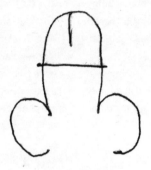

Here we have a
standard speednob, with
two balls, a retracted
foreskin, and a piss-eye.

First, we have 'Rudey the
Backwards Chef'. His hat crafted
from testicles, and the urethra
forms an attractive chin dimple.
No one could be offended by
Rudey, even if his name *is* Rudey.

Next, we have a Norman
soldier. To fully hide the
testicles, your soldier will
need a sword *and* a shield,
like a real Norman soldier
would have.

Finally, we have an admirable
model of religious tolerance. A Jew,
a Catholic and a Sikh, just chillin'
together. This could actually win
you favour with more easily
delightable teachers.

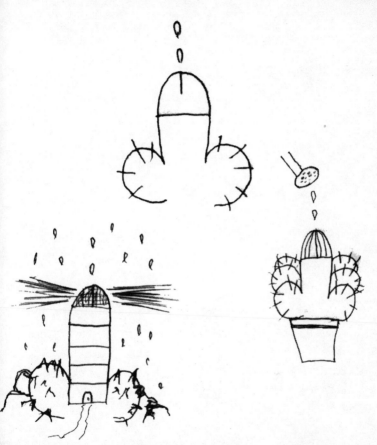

If your artist has managed to draw spunk and pubes, then your task is more difficult. The cactus and watering can is semi-convincing, despite it not looking that much like a cactus; but the lighthouse scene should fox even the most cock-suspicious of teachers, who can now only tell you off for drawing lighthouses in your book.

135

O o

old teacher in the cupboard, there is an Get one classmate to hide in a cupboard. Then convince your victim that the teacher is in the cupboard, that he is very cross, and that he wants to see him.

Then, when the victim is safely locked in the cupboard, the other boy should hurl ink and paper at him, and shout such teacherly things as '*YOU, BOY!*'

Lots of fun for those outside the cupboard, who get to hear the shouting and watch a cupboard rattle around for a bit. *See also: you, boy!*

one for the ladies A section in *Razzle* where the male readers sent in naked pictures of themselves, presumably so that they could show the wife, to try and get her in the mood.

Although *Razzle* paid £10 for every '*one for the ladies*' entry they used, children with dollar signs in their eyes would be well advised that *Razzle* rarely – if ever – used a photo of a pre-pubescent 13-year-old boy. Even if he was wearing a balaclava so that his mum wouldn't recognise him.

OOOOOOWWWW Prefix to an insult. Should be said in the voice of Henry's

Cat. Replaces unmanageable sentences; can also be used to drown out any interruptions or retorts of your opponent.

A: Well at least I ...

B: Oooooowwww, bronno ...

A: At leas ...

B: Oooooowwww ...

A: At ...

B: (louder) ... wwwwwwwww

A: A ...

B: (louder) ... WWWWWWWW

Whilst making the *oooooowwww* noise, Child B may run off before he runs out of breath, denying Child A the chance to reply between '*oooooowwww*'s.

operation pickfords
On the last day of school, stay up all night, moving all of the bins and benches from school on to the field and using them to spell out a naughty word, such as potty, or bum.

operation sex
To the theme tune of 'Catch The Pigeon'.

> *Operation, Operation,*
> *Operation, Operation,*
> *Operation, Operation, SEX! (awoo)*

'Where Dastardly would say "awoo", the instigators of *Operation Sex* would jump and thrust groins into mid-air at some bemused girls. *Operation Sex* continued for three years. Then, as suddenly as it started, it ended. Was it deemed a success on debriefing? I wonder.'

orchestra, willy

> *Bum Tit Tit! Bum Tit Tit!*
> *Turn the hairy handle now,*
> *Bum Tit Tit! Bum Tit Tit!*
> *Hear the willy orchestra.*

The hairy handle was often accompanied by the fanny banjo. **See also: fanjo**

ordeals, unconvincing
To demonstrate how hard you are, claim that you can grip the hardest on a thorny stalk. Then look as indignantly agonised as you can, whilst maintaining the loosest possible grip on the thorns.

Other 'hard nut' tests involved trying to karate chop stupidly thick branches, and stealing Mrs Rich's hairspray.

or9 Getting caught desk-writing can leave you in an impossible quandary.

'I was trying to write "SEX ORGY", but sensing trouble I scratched out "SEX" and left "ORGY" half-finished. At the end of the class the teacher approached my desk and read "ORG" and then asked if I was trying to write "ORC", assuming I was a fantasy-reading Dungeons & Dragons fan.

'I had to choose between Orgy and Orc, and to my eternal shame, I falsely confessed to being a D&D fan. One of the lowest moments in my life.'

origami love/attack thing Here is a guide for anyone wanting to tell their friends they fancy Luke Goss, or attack someone.

1. Take a sheet of A4. Take the bottom left corner and fold it at 45 degrees so that the bottom side runs exactly along the right side. Cut off the redundant strip of paper that runs along the top. Fold across the other way to create an 'X' in folds. The 'X' should intersect at the centre of the square. **2.** Fold all four corners 'A' in, so that the points meet at the centre. **3.** Turn the sheet over. Fold all four corners 'B' into the centre, as before. **4.** Fold over line C then unfold line C again (this will make the final stage easier), then fold over line D. **5.** You should now notice four slots, or flaps, in one side. Put a thumb and finger of each hand into these slots, or flaps. Pinch together, and with some jiggling the creature should fall into shape. *See illustrations overleaf.*

Girls: Write hidden fortunes on the inside flaps, including whether Luke Goss loves you (not his icky identical twin, Matt).

Boys: Draw eyes and a tongue on the creature and use it to attack your friends' faces, all the time saying *'No! What are you doing? Leave him alone!'* to your unruly pet.

ostracise A word that you first learn when you are being told off for doing it.

If there is a child called Andrew Bard in your class, and you sing 'Ooh-ah, Andrew Beard, I say ooh-ah Andrew Beard', you are 'ostracising' him.

O ORIGAMI LOVE/ATTACK THING

1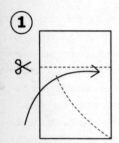

STEP ONE: If you don't have square paper, and are using A4, fold one corner of the paper to the opposite side, creating a 45 degree fold. This will show the line you have to cut across to make a square.

2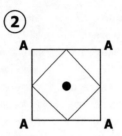

STEP TWO: Fold all corners of the square into the centre, along the diagonal lines shown.

3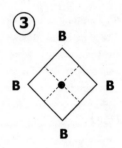

STEP THREE: Turn the paper over, then fold the corners into the centre again. Note that the dotted lines in this diagram are entirely unhelpful.

4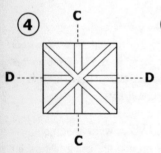

STEP FOUR: Your paper should look a bit like this now. Fold along line C, unfold, fold along line D, unfold, then fold again on line C to get to stage five.

5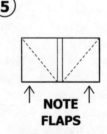

NOTE FLAPS

STEP FIVE: Note the four individual flaps. Stick one finger in each, then kinda wiggle it around a bit.

6

STEP SIX: Hey presto. An origami (except for the scissors bit at the beginning) thing that you can use to find out who someone loves. Or to attack someone's face.

'In retrospect the charge of ostracism was a little unfair – Andrew was in no way excluded from the opportunity to join in. In fact, his surname wasn't even Beard, it was Bard, so I don't know what anyone was complaining about.'

overhead projector It's always good to see smoke and fumes coming out of things. In the case of the overhead projector, this could be achieved by pushing thin blue plastic straws into the cooling fan.

Oxby Coat 'Any filthy, discarded or "used" coat or shirt, preferably found in the street. The Oxby Coat would be picked up and thrown at the victim, who had to wear it if it so much as touched them. Everyone else would then shout "Oxby!" until … well, until we stopped, I suppose.'

P p

packets don't come in tins Retort for a bully who is told to 'pack it in' during his abuse. Your lunatic suggestion that packets *do* come in tins will only enrage him further.

pacman The sound that PacMan makes when running around his maze is 'wacca wacca wacca', like a triple-speed Fozzie Bear. Make this sound when you see someone being chased, and the bully might pause from his pursuit and say, 'Do you mind? You're rendering my chase faintly absurd.'

page 215 The forever-to-be-remembered page number in one biology textbook featuring a photograph of a standing naked child with the most extraordinary bow legs. This relegated to second place the illustrations of *In the Night Kitchen* (Maurice Sendak), which had a drawing of a naked boy standing on a giant milk bottle, shouting 'Cock A Doodle Doo'.

pain relief experiments The only Nazi experiment to filter down to the playground. You would have the crap beaten out of you, the aforementioned crap being beaten *scientifically* out of the areas most likely to cause severe pain.

Just when you approached the threshold of tolerable pain, your shoes were scientifically torn off and thrown away, and your tormentors would *scientifically* pummel the soles of your feet, to test the postulated theory that this cancelled out pain anywhere else in your body.

So that you don't have to find out for yourself, the results are no, it doesn't cancel out the pain everywhere else in your body. It honestly doesn't.

pal Personal Arse Licker. Never say that you are someone's pal; 'best pal' is a bit better, because it implies that there is some competition for the job, and at least you're a *good* arse licker.

palm reading The traditional and tedious method of palm reading – pretending to see the person's house, the driveway and all their cars, and then gobbing on to their palm to create the swimming pool – is lent a little more credibility if you hock up an over-sized greeny, and inform them that they have problems with the pool filter.

For the less mucally minded, simply ask someone if they want their palm read, and if they say yes, daub them with a red felt marker. Alternatively, ask someone if they can read palms – and whatever they reply, show them the words 'YOU ARE A COCK' written cheerfully across your palm.

pantomime rehearsals, erotic 'The teacher who directed our primary-school pantomime used to put a lot of effort into after-school rehearsals. Sometimes just for one or two of the cast, singled out as the star performers.

'At one such personal session, Abanazar the wicked uncle (played by myself) and Widow Twanky were encouraged to lie down on our backs, side by side, in just our PE kit, and let our hands "explore" each other's bodies without making a sound. We were told that this would teach us "proper body control". The teacher turned the light off and watched us do it in silence for about 10 minutes. My parents thought he was a wonderful teacher and refused to listen to any complaint.

'I thought this was going to be a funny story, but it appears to have taken me to a very dark place.'

pants check police

A group whose privileges include checking underwear in the changing rooms during swimming lessons. If they found a poo stripe, they were then entitled to take the underwear to the side of the pool and declare, for example, 'Eur, Connor's got poo stripes.'

parka

The act of swinging a smaller child by the fur-trimmed hood of their Lord Anthony parka until it rips, the child squirms free, you get tired arms or boredom sets in.

More fun can be had by tying the parka's cords to the metal bars on the bus home, giving the wearer two choices – lose the coat, or take an unplanned trip to town and miss *Chocky's Children*.

parted, two cows went up the hill and

The phrase '*two cows went up the hill and parted*' is magically transformed if you put a finger in each side of your mouth and pull your cheeks apart. As is '*my dad's a banker*'.

pascal the bear wrestler

A fairly shit, if slightly charming, song, sung to the tune of 'Go West'.

> *Pascal, wrestles grizzly bears,*
> *Pascal, in the open air.*
> *Pascal, in his underwear.*
> *Pascal, that's why we don't care.*

'If we were really so indifferent to Pascal's habits, however, it's odd that we spent so much time singing about how much we didn't care. Methinks we did protest too much.'

peanut shootout

A game for peanut-allergy sufferers. The boy with the allergy puts his mouth at the end of the table. Other boys try to flick peanuts into his mouth. He is allowed to use a Coke bottle as a goalkeeper.

That same child can also play Revels

Russian Roulette. One in six Revels contains a peanut. Because the peanut Revels have the most distinctive shape, this game is more fun if your victim doesn't realise that you're offering Revels, or you simply force them into his face.

pe in your pants Forgetting your kit would result in PE in your pants. PE in your pants sounds a bit like pee in your pants, but it isn't.

pencil suicide Urban Myth, Part One. Young man, overcome with stress, puts a pencil up either nostril during an exam and brings his head down on the desk. The pencils go into his brain, killing him instantly. Urban Myth, Part Two. Everyone in the room gets an A.

'I actually became good friends with someone a couple of years ago who claimed to have been in the room at the time of the "incident". When I met him, he could barely talk due to severe drug abuse over the preceding years, and he had a genuine fear of pencils – he was fine with pens but pencils would make

him start shaking and crying. I should point out again, perhaps, the severe drug abuse.'

pencils, other fun with Sharpen a graphite pencil at both ends, and then clip the power supply connectors to the exposed lead. The graphite core becomes searingly hot – and stays so for ages. Then leave out for the bullying tart who belittled your knowledge of physics as being 'swotty' and watch the blisters form on her chubby little fingers when she (as usual) helps herself to your writing tools. Resistors aren't futile!

pen fifteen club You have 15 pens in an exciting variety of styles and hues. So do all the other members. It's a whole bunch of fun. Who WOULDN'T want to be in the Pen Fifteen Club? So the uncool kid, desperate to join the gang, collects together 15 pens in an equally exciting variety of styles and hues, and proudly presents them to the club. 'Brilliant!' you tell him. 'You have 15 pens! Now you can receive the secret Pen Fifteen Club sign!' Taking the biggest, blackest and most indelible of your collection, you then write 'PEN 15' in big letters on said kid's hand.

A nice way of dealing with the kind of child who actually *does* collect pens or scented rubbers.

penis corner

A more elaborate and good-natured version of *speednob*. Cut off a corner segment of blank paper, and draw a crude phallus. When your classmate's back is turned, place your corner of paper over the corner of his work, with a carefully placed ruler hiding the join.

After your friend has noticed the ruination of his work and let fly with a suitably outraged volley of insults, you can slide the paper away and reveal that it was all a joke. Relief generally diffuses anger, and a jolly good laugh is had by all, before retiring to the drawing room with a tall glass of Dandelion & Burdock.

penny burns

Something the hard lads at school devoted much time and effort to achieve. By vigorously rubbing the skin on the back of your hand with a two pence piece (tails down was more effective) you could friction-burn away the top few layers of skin. When repeated enough times this would lead to a much-admired thick brown scab about a centimetre wide and over an inch long.

Well-burned children may develop forearms like Tony the Tiger's hind legs.

Also consider *biro burns*. Furiously scribble a biro in the back of a textbook or on a bit of cardboard for a few minutes then press the hot nib into the skin on the back of your hand to give yourself an everlasting freckle.

See also: pus bubble wars

period party bag

All the girls of a certain age got these party bags, and also got to see a film called *Becoming a Woman*. Boys, having no equivalent fun pack for their puberty, became quite jealous of this very visible rite of adulthood.

In better-natured schools, the girls would share their free tampons and join with the boys in a game of *wet the tampon with liquid soap and throw it at the ceiling*.

pe teachers, work avoidance for

1. 'Run to the wall and back': translates to 'I can't be arsed. Run to the wall and back, while I stand here with my hands deep enough into my pockets to play with myself.'

2. 'Play amongst yourselves': Most sport is self-regulating, and doesn't really need a teacher watching it – sit in the staff room and let the little bastards sort it out themselves. Maintain a sense of professionalism by occasionally nipping in, blowing a whistle and shouting a surname.

3. 'The 12-Minute Run': shuts children up for exactly 12 minutes. This allows the PE teacher to stare into the middle distance and meditate on where everything went wrong.

4. Open gym, leave the equipment room unlocked, watch a quoit-filled re-enactment of *Lord of the Flies*.

phantom shit spreader

If someone shits in the urinal, on the floor and up the walls, it is amazing the lengths to which a teacher will go in order not to say 'someone has shat up the walls'. Amongst the phrases employed to avoid saying the word 'shit' or 'toilet' will be ...

'We have a very serious problem.'

'You all know what I'm talking about.'

'There has been an inappropriate use of the facilities.'

'The culprit certainly knows what I'm talking about.'

'I hope this will never happen again, because if something like this should ever reoccur, measures will have to be taken.'

philately

The askee is asked: 'Do you collect stamps?' If he says yes, his foot is stamped upon.

A more sophisticated variant is to ask the question: 'Do you want a Shakespeare Stamp?' If he says yes, shake him, 'spear' (punch) him in the chest and stamp on his feet. If he says no, tell him that he obviously does want one, then shake him, spear him and stamp on his feet.

pig If anyone calls you a pig, and you are a girl, then you can claim that it stands for 'pretty, intelligent girl'. Make sure you emphasise the pause, so it is clear that you're pretty *and* intelligent, and not just kinda pretty intelligent.

pile on! Also known as a 'bundle'. If someone falls over on the hard gravel floor of the playground, anyone is entitled to scream '*pile on!*' and everyone is then obliged to jump on top of them. *Pile-ons* can also be arranged so the person is pushed to the ground. *Pile-ons* often lead to serious injuries and writhing homoeroticism.

pinch-punch, first of the month The application of a *nipple gripple* and dead arm on the first day of the month to the chant of '*Pinch-Punch, First of the Month*'.

The proper retort to this was an appreciative 'A punch and a kick for being so quick'. If the initiator didn't like his punch

and kick, then he could administer 'a poke in the eye for being so sly'.

pinfinger The painless insertion of a pin under a layer of dead skin on the fingertip. Experts can manage 10 pinfingers without accidentally popping one out. This leaves the pinfingerer able to do very little, other than wave their fingers eerily at people and say 'Look! Look! *Pinfingers!*'

pink and blasphemous The role-playing game of Call of Cthulhu is based loosely on the works of H.P. Lovecraft, and is designed to instil fear and dread into its players. Dungeon Mastering such games carried its own risks.

'In my third year of secondary school, I was leading a few mates in a game of Cthulhu. Getting caught up in the atmosphere, I made the terrible mistake of saying that one of the beasts the team had encountered was "*pink and blasphemous*", within earshot of a school bully. That bully's ponce-dar went off the scale, and I was hounded by cries of "*pink and blasphe-mous*" until the day I left that school, five years later.'

pink floyd Liking Pink Floyd before a certain age of maturity (35) will single you out as a bender.

piss flaps A *joystick-waggler* game for the Atari ST, created by the lovable Hot Spunk Crew.

Each level began with a sample from Jack Nicholson as The Joker in *Batman*, saying '*Gentlemen – let's broaden our minds*', after which you would immediately thrash your joystick from left to right. This action would animate one of a series of very short films, which included a bean-flicking incident and some hot three-way pixels.

Although obviously a humorous game invented by Dutchmen far more used to pornography than ourselves, it was immensely frustrating if you actually did want to wank, as the action stopped if you let up with your joystick hand. You *could* convince a friend to waggle the joystick for you; but if

you're that comfortable in each other's company you might as well just toss each other off anyway.

piss shower If you smelled very bad then it could be suggested that you showered by standing under a colander that your father was pissing into with his scabby penis.

piss tissue To play *piss tissue*, soak a hefty wad of toilet roll in the urinal or trough, hoke it out with a stick and sling it over a cubicle door at anyone stupid enough to be dropping brown in the school toilet.

His immediate instinct will be to stand up and retaliate, or at least get the piss tissue off him. The secondary instinct to remain seated, to avoid mid-bob clench and smearing, will create a panicked tension.

pissy circle Where everyone stands along the urinals in the PE block. One shouts '*pissy circle*' and does a swift pirouette, sending a looping strand of piss over his co-pissers.

Alternatively, slip your hands through the crooks of a smaller child's arms whilst he is pissing, lift him up and spin him around, thus drenching all other kids in the immediate vicinity. Minutes of fun.

pitch black kung fu

Kung Fu performed in total darkness. One of the more dangerous forms of Kung Fu, especially in the hands of clumsy jumping juveniles whose only experience of martial arts is 'backwards and fire does a roundhouse kick on Way of the Exploding Fist'.

Battles last around five minutes, after which people will be bruised and breathless, unless someone has watched Van Damme's *Bloodsport*, in which case noses will get broken.

playboy/playgirl

Ask the victim whether they like *Playboy* or *Playgirl*.

The brief confusion, that *Playgirl* is for boys, and *Playboy* is for girls, will allow you to scream that they're not sure whether they like boys or girls, and must therefore be 170% gay.

playground pornography, the economics of

A keen opportunity for the playground entrepreneur.

Copy of low-quality jazz mag	£2
Pages in low-quality jazz mag	50
Individual resale value of page	20p
Near instant profit	£8

'In an ingenious twist, I sold the pages by a raffle mechanism, whereby the purchaser would "pick a number". Thus, pages without pornography were simply "unlucky" rather than "unsellable".

'Obviously, there were certain overheads to be accounted for – for example, the cut you'd have to give your elder brother to buy the magazine in the first place. However, these were easily outweighed by the cachet gained from being the school's answer to Hugh Hefner.' *See also: porn baron*

plop stones

During breaktime, collect a few large stones. Inform a peer that you are about to have a shit in the pond, then drop the stones behind your back, slightly squatting, making ever-increasingly tortured straining noises before each is released. When boredom sets in, perform the same trick to the girls.

PLP If you admit that you are a PLP, then you're a Public Leaning Post, and the person who asked you if you are a PLP will lean on your head. Say no, and you're denying that you're a Perfectly Lovely Person. Why would anyone deny that he was a perfectly lovely person? You'd have to be an idiot.

polaroids, fun with, biscuit-related Take a Jammy Dodger biscuit, put it on the edge of the table, whip out your willy and take a Polaroid of your member touching the biscuit.

Take the packet of Jammy Dodgers into school. Offer them around, with an assurance that they haven't been spat on. The second the biscuit is in their mouth, show them the Polaroid.

The photo is good for around three packets of Jammy Dodgers before word gets around that it's a joke. Or that you're the guy who puts his dick on Jammy Dodgers.

Warning: This will not work with a regular camera because the lab will call the police and you will be arrested for fucking a nostalgic biscuit.

polo Acronym for *pants off, legs open*. A general term for a slapper. Alternatively, *penis out, legs open* which is a general term for drawn-out foreplay.

polo challenge A full packet of Polo mints had to be eaten outright, against the clock (ending with a mouth inspection for illegal residue). Crunching was the only stipulation with no full-mint gulping allowed, and the packet was usually split open beforehand to allow for quicker access. Manic chomping on a gob full of brittle mint shards invariably resulted in lacerated gums, chipped teeth, loss of fillings, etc., but a small price to pay for a shot at the coveted title, currently standing at 21.3 seconds.

polyvelts One of Clark's Shoes' better-thought-out products. By not including any form of grips or tread on the bottom of the shoe, they created the perfect shoe for winter skids. Desperately unsafe – hats off to shoes from Clark's for giving children what they want.

poo bag, matthew has a

'When a child in our year was lucky enough to have a colostomy bag, the school in their wisdom decided that an assembly would be the best way to promote understanding. And so it was that hundreds of five-year-olds came to learn that Matthew carried his poo around in a bag all day.

'So, we thought, if Michael collected poo in his bag, he might want *our* poos for his bag, too. We didn't like the sound of this. We were horrified that he would even *think* about collecting our poos in such a way. So one chronically ill child became a chronically ill outcast.'

poo dance

If you've found a dog poo on the way home from school, but are bored of the *poo game*, why not go solo and bedazzle your friends with a flamboyant *poo dance*?

Based on the (pooless) Scottish sword dance, the protagonist cavorts above the poo to the strains of a pretend bagpipe. Points are awarded for technical complexity and how close the shoes get to the poo without touching it.

The game ends if the dancer stands in the poo. Or, if it is a dry poo, kicks it at a spectator. *See also: poo game*

poo game

Walking home from school with your mates? Found a nice fresh dog poo? Then you have all you need to play the *poo game*.

Stand face to face with your combatant, the poo between you, and link hands over it. The aim of the game is to push and pull your opponent until he steps in the poo.

Best practised when your mate is wearing new shoes with good, deep treads (not *polyvelts*). Also known as 'poomo wrestling'. *See also: poo dance*

poo on a stick

An amusing but dangerous game. Placing a firm but internally succulent poo on a stick, run headlong at someone, with the shitty

end of the stick as far away from you as possible, shouting, '*Eeuugghh … poo on a stick!*' Alternatively, just fire it at some unsuspecting passer-by with absolutely no warning. Then shout, '*Poo on a stick*', to let them know what happened.
See also: shit sticks

poof-way arch A road sign supported by two pillars straddling the pavement just outside a particular school entrance. Any person who inadvertently walked between the pillars was destined to lifelong homosexuality unless they could retrace their steps within three seconds. If walking this stretch of pavement with a friend, you would attempt to engage them in protracted and intense conversation so that you would both walk through the arch. Then wait, like holding a grenade, and run back through the archway, reclaiming your heterosexuality, leaving your friend doomed to eternal gaymosex.

popper A gay male. Possibly derived from the sphincter-loosening drug Amyl Nitrate, although possibly from the sound that we imagined bumsex made. Intense sessions must have sounded like rolling in bubblewrap.

porn baron One child in every generation is destined to find the balance between pariah and popularity. The company of one anaemic child will be suffered more than the others. This child will either have a newsagent or a pervert in the family, or be a shoplifter. And lo, his collection of pornography shall be immense. And he shall deliver this pornography to chosen ones, those to whom *nearly knickers* has been a genuine torture for too many years. And these people will kinda stare at it, hold it at different angles until they're sure they're supposed to be that way up, and probably wank a bit, if they've worked out how.
See also: nearly knickers

porn breaks A brief break during any lesson, devoted to miming your favourite sex act. Declared by the loud command of 'porn break', loud enough for all the members of the class to hear. Props were allowed – including chairs, tables, cupboards, bins and board rubbers. *Porn breaks* lasted for a maximum of five seconds, after which everyone sat down and carried on working in complete silence as if nothing had ever happened.

posting A torture often inflicted for minor infractions of playground rule, such as not being popular. The victim is held by the legs by two people, who then run as fast as they can towards a suitable post (usually a goal post, hence the name, but occasionally a tree, fence, etc). The two draggers run either side of the post, causing massive testicular damage to the dragee.

This is also known as '*scroating*' if you've read books about what bits of the cock are called.

posting, extreme 'At my school, posting was perfected to achieve a more painful end. The "postee" was carried by four "posters" so more speed could be developed, and was posted face down into one of the thick wooden struts which support cricket sightscreens. These, for those not in the know, slope downwards at approximately 45 degrees, thus ensuring maximum contact twixt post and genitalia.'

posting, pressurised A variant on standard posting which would involve grabbing your victim's legs while they were astride some section of climbing frame. You would then recruit as much help as possible (sometimes three pullers to one leg) and pull the victim's legs towards you and hence crush his genitals against the climbing frame. The net result of all of this was that the boys never went on the climbing frames. The girls couldn't either, because all of the boys would look up their skirts. Therefore, the climbing frames became the exclusive domain of the ugly girls.

pot pourri A decorative form of pot. Smoked by desperate children who have yet to develop connections into the drugs underworld. This echoes other sad attempts to get high, including dried banana skins and microwaved menthol Tunes.

'One child misunderstood the intricacies of the banana skin trick and grilled an entire banana. He then tried to smoke the charred remains in some sort of perverse Groucho Marx parody.'

pressure points Any point on the human body which, when jabbed by the fingers of someone who has attended two Kung Fu classes, will cause collapse, haemorrhaging and eventual death.

pubic spliff A legal yet distasteful rolled cigarette, made out of pubic hair and pubic hair alone.

puddingbowl lane If Tuppenywhore Lane is where your mum lives, then Puddingbowl Lane is where you get your hair cut.

puma A convenient label, incorporated into clothing, that the wearer is a *poof under medical attention*.

purple cloud An unpopular female music teacher with dark hair one day appeared to have dyed it slightly purple. When asked how that came to be, she replied, '*I walked under a purple cloud, and it rained!*'

This 'joke' was met with howls of laughter so transparently sarcastic that the teacher was humiliated. Well, for the first minute, anyway. After the fake laughter went on for 10 more minutes, she just burst into tears and ran from the room.

Teachers — don't be funny unless you're also scary.

purple nurple A two-handed *nipple gripple*. It should also be much harder than the *nipple gripple*, so that the nipples turn a gruesome shade of purple. The *nipple gripple* can be used for fun — the *purple nurple* is for punishment only.

pus bubble wars To show who is supatuff, hold each other's hands down and use a pencil eraser to burn a large skinless hole in your hand, by spinning the eraser back and forth as hard as possible on one spot on the top of your hand – like starting a fire with a stick.

Bonus round! While the wound was healing it would normally grow a bubble full of pus. Smack the bubbles of fellow supatuff pupils, and bathe in the yellow spatter. *See also: penny burns*

quaid 'After the release of *Total Recall*, we happily had a kid in our year called Quaid, the name of Arnold's hero in the film.

'It became something of a routine to imitate the alien mutant's cries of "Quaaaaaaaaid" until he started crying. One such session was made especially notable when his older brother found him crying. We thought we were in trouble when he asked him why he was so upset. When little Quaid said, "They keep calling me Quaid," big Quaid simply replied, "It's your name, you stupid dick," and punched him in the face.'

quegg A pubeless male individual who has showered in the company of more virile boys and been seen for the queggy girl that he is.

Possibly a melding of queer (because you are) and egg (because that's what your balls look like).

questionable fantasies as education 'We were told by our Latin teacher that a popular punishment in Roman times was to insert a fish into the rectum head first and pull it out. When pulled out, the scales of the fish, which lay one way, would open out and cause irreparable damage to the luckless anus. He also told us that a similar thing was done with radishes. When we questioned the realistic punishment value of inserting such an evidently small and friendly vegetable he explained that "radishes were different then, all big and spiny like a pineapple". This caused us to consider whether anything he actually said was true, or whether our education was simply comprised of a number of our teacher's more questionable fantasies.'

quiz? eggo! veins! A method of distributing unwanted goods.

At the end of the year, when kids were clearing out their desks and didn't want stuff any more, they would hold up an item and shout 'Quiz!' The first kid to respond with a yell of 'Eggo!' was given the item. The bidding could get fast and furious, but shouting 'Eggo!' prematurely was inadvisable, in case you got a gym sock or a dirty syringe. If you did get such a dirty prize, then you could give it back only if the donor hadn't shouted 'Veins!'

The fact that this whole affair is conducted in Latin makes it a distastefully intellectual affair. In normal schools, simply throw things you don't want at someone you don't mind hurting.

quoits A joyless rubber hoop from really early PE classes, where they didn't think you capable of using something so wildly complex as a ball. Accompanied by little bean bags that can in no way be fruitfully used in conjunction with the quoits. Can be explained in Roman Catholic schools in that balls are considered too much fun, and sexy. Bouncing around like that. Phaw.

R r

racing cars This game is good for children with low self-control. A simple variant on the classic humming game, which has confounded teachers for a century. *Racing cars* started, as usual, with a low crescendo of humming.

However, when the teacher became aware of the humming, instead of shutting up, players must roar as loudly as possible, mimicking whichever vehicle – or animal – they damn well please. Pupils could run around the classroom, too, if they liked.

radiator skin A team effort requiring patience, a streaming cold and a strong stomach.

By coating a radiator with snot and phlegm and leaving it to bake hard, it is possible to 'grow', over the course of a few weeks, a material akin to snake-skin. Further prosthetic enhancements (especially ears and lips) can be made from the Hubba Bubba mountains on the undersides of the desks.

Once it has been properly cultivated, all you need to do then is find someone on whom to perform a makeover.

rage, the Only certain children are capable of achieving the rage. It is the state where you are given superhuman strength by two silver lines of snot running from your nose to your mouth. Once this bionic power feed is broken, the child will lose their powers and become sullen, sorry and somewhat confused at the chaos that surrounds them.

raggers Unpopular children who would come to school with bags full of sweets in a pathetic attempt to ingratiate themselves with the more popular, infinitely richer and therefore fundamentally better kids.

The dilemma – sweets are nice, but talking to the *ragger* is not going to do you any social favours. The solution? Take the bag and offer them around yourself.

rainbow puffs Small multi-coloured puffed sugar rice. On sale at the breaktime tuck shop for 5p a bag, they contained enough E-numbers to fell a mechanical horse. Guaranteed to induce raging spasms, violent behaviour and epileptic fits in anyone fortunate enough to try some. And that's before you even get started on the name.

rambo, but i'm Not a convincing reason why you shouldn't be sent to the headmaster's office for pointing a replica pistol at the caretaker. Also '*Don't push me, I'm muscly*'.

rape, misinterpretation of 'Perhaps based on the word "rapier", I thought for some time that the term "rape" meant to attack someone with a knife. I rather foolishly enquired with a group of male friends whether or not we should go rape the girls. Happily I wasn't waving a knife around at the time … that would have been alarming.'

The teller of this story seems charmingly unaware of how unacceptable it is to go around stabbing girls.

rectal prolapse The musical variant of the game of *fuck*. Instead of shouting louder and louder, the first player sings '*Rectal Prolapse*' in as low a tone as he can and holds the last note. The next player picks this up a few tones higher. This arpeggio continues until the full musical range of the group has been covered. On some occasions, this is musically quite pleasant. **See also: fuck**

red ender Achieved by daubing a little tomato ketchup on the front of your grey trousers, and running your crotch into seated girls' faces. They might not get what's going on, so explain; say, '*I've got a red ender.*' Not to be confused with period envy.
See: period party bags

rem Short for remedial, a common insult. Extra mileage could be squeezed from the tube by grasping the handles of an invisible motorbike and starting it up, as though on a cold day. 'Remmm. Remmememem. REMememememEMEMEMEM (twist throttle), REEEEMMMM! Reeeeeeemmm, reeeeeemmmm, rerrrrmmmmm.' And so on.

This was not insulting the mentally ill, it was merely making motorbike noises near them, and *rems* could even join in – they *love* motorbikes and fast noisy stuff like that.

rent-a-tent Hypothetical shop. Where fat girls get their dresses.

rescue squadron 'Being a member of Rescue Squadron involved swarming upon a small group of people in the playground and pushing them around a bit, then we'd all run off, spin around and shout "*Rescue Squadron*". This was us "transforming". When we'd totally transformed we'd run back to our original victims and pretend to rescue them from their attackers (who had mysteriously disappeared). Our rescue involved jumping on them again, but this time shouting "*Rescue Squadron!*"

'Eventually the year above formed "Playground Patrol" to protect pupils from Rescue Squadron.'

resistance is useless A large mob of kids would gather round a solitary victim. Placing one hand on the victim's shoulder, it would be solemnly announced that 'resistance is useless'.

Then, they would be led to a 15-foot-deep ditch in an isolated area of the yard and hurled in. The game became a deep test of character for the victim. Some would try to run, some would claw the ground and scream for help that never came, but others would raise their heads high and walk slowly and with dignity to the waiting abyss.

This last approach was often accompanied by a round of applause from the mob, whose appreciation of such mettle stopped just short of not throwing the person in the pit.

resusci-annie 'Resusci-Annie

was an unpleasant-tasting plastic torso. When it rained during PE, we were made to practise resuscitation techniques upon her. Eventually, the congealed spittle of a thousand children made her go mouldy and she was deposited in a skip. And there it should end.

'We rescued her, and dressed her in a cast-off uniform from Lost Property. We put her in bins, in lockers, and

eventually hung her from a tree by her little plastic neck. This caused a teacher to faint and for Annie to be incinerated.'

revels russian roulette
See: peanut shootout

rhymes, skipping If you have

excluded a girl from skipping, then you may make the skipping rhymes relate to how many dollops of poo she did. Good skippers could have the excluded girl doing hundreds of dollops of poo, and if she's going to do that much poo she doesn't *deserve* to have anyone talking to her.

ridley The most basic form of retort

to an insult, named after one of its most vociferous proponents:

A: You're crap.

Ridley: No, *you're* crap.

This retort, requiring no brainpower at all, is worse than *emery dermis, egg dribble*, and *sly old fox*. They're all shit, but at least the boy who said 'egg dribble' was *trying*.

robbie is a laura 'The endless chants and badges made for Robbie, when – in a horrific accident of classroom seating arrangements – he ended up sat with three Lauras. From that point on, Robbie was a Laura.'

robert's apples 'Replying to Robert's comment that our experiment was giving off a smell like apples, our Scottish chemistry teacher piped up, "Well, I wouldn't mind some of your apples, Robert!" This was greeted with a stunned silence.'

roger the dinosaur 'With a head composed of my middle finger and legs forged from the other four fingers, Roger the Dinosaur was the absolute smash of the class, until some attention-seeking *loser* offered to chew ink cartridges for 20p.'

ron dodo penis Dada-ist alteration of the phrase 'Front Windows Do Not Open', as seen on the top deck of the school bus. Requires some time, and a marker pen to complete the word

'penis'. ***See also: executive will press for highest penalties against offenders, the***

rubber balls and liquor
A: After every question I ask, say 'rubber balls and liquor'.
B: Okay.
A: What did you eat for breakfast?
B: Rubber balls and liquor.
A: What did you eat for lunch?
B: Rubber balls and liquor.
A: What are you going to eat for dinner?
B: Rubber balls and liquor.
A: What are you going to do to your girlfriend tonight?
B: Rubber balls and liquor.
It was, at least, good to know that Child B had come to terms with his girlfriend's pair of enormous vulcanised balls.

rubber penises Write 'rubber penises' on a sticker, and apply it to a drawer or filing cabinet. Then, entice someone into opening the drawer.
When they do, feign disgust and say,

'Eur, you're looking for a rubber penis. You've been hunting high and low for it. You're in love with a rubber penis.'

rubbers on radiators Quietly placing a rubber on a scorching radiator at the beginning of the lesson will create a miniature junkyard 'stack of flaming tyres' stench. By the time it reaches the front of the class and the teacher becomes aware of it, the room is utterly full of stank, three rows of children have fallen off their chairs and there's nothing anyone can do.

ruler smelling 'I'm not sure whether this has a name to it, but I remember licking the end of my ruler, then making someone else smell it. I suppose this might come under the heading "Ruler Smelling", were it to be included in a dictionary.'

S s

sac attack A minor form of flashing for the sexually unembarrassed. Simply carry out everyday life, with your testicles hanging out of your trousers. For a more aggressive sac attack, you could try running up to a pensioner and getting your testicles out.

saint and greavsie's chase up the channel

Improbable board game, linking ITV's erstwhile top sports presenters with the true story of how the Spanish Armada foundered on the rocks around the coasts of Britain. Surprisingly, it was deemed of sufficient historical value

that its creators were forced to play it on school open night in front of the bewildered parents of prospective pupils.

sam A speech synthesis programme on the Commodore 64 that allowed you to say that anyone in your class had bad breath, and wore a wig due to the fact that they were gay and shagged male cats.

satanism, junior Most children will experiment at some point with Satanism.

During a game of ten-pin bowling, children praying for a strike may briefly

switch to praying to Satan for a couple of frames, to see if his prayers are answered any more efficiently.

Children will also play with ouija boards in the attic, where ghosts live. Ouija boards will generally spell three-quarters of a swear word before someone asks who is pushing it.

Other children will half-heartedly doodle pentagrams on their jotters, not realising that the *real* way to raise Lucifer from the pit is to have a load of kids all link pinkies in a big circle, close their eyes and chant '*Satan come and scratch us*'. Satan would then take time out from his busy schedule of war-mongering and globalisation to scratch a child a little bit on their face.

Other Satan-summoning techniques involved placing 10p on a grave at midnight and dancing around it ten times. One nervous attempt to recreate these conditions involved using a green fruit

Ouija board
This board contains all the words you will need to use the ouija with your friends. The numbers have been included so you can find out how many times Steve's mother has shagged your RE teacher.

pastille and dancing round it five times at midday. Nothing happened.

Elsewhere, one acolyte of darkness informed us that he planned to stay awake until midnight and recite the Lord's Prayer backwards, in the hopes of conjuring up Beelzebub himself. When he didn't turn up at school the next day we were naturally concerned that the Devil had stolen poor Andy away. Luckily he'd just overslept, having stayed up past his bedtime on a school night.

sausage, continental

'The distinction between the French words 'saucisson' and 'saucissez', according to the *Tricolore* books, is that one was a 'continental' sausage. I have not heard this expression since I was 11, and my endless requests for continental sausage in the local Co-op have met with a stony indifference. It did, however, form the basis of my first bilingual song:

> *Continental sausage /*
> *continental sausage.*
> *Continental sausage / je suis!*

sausages, education through talking

'German textbooks were narrated by a talking sausage. Enterprising young men – well, everyone really – would draw a line across and a line down, ensuring that German was taught to following years by a cock in lederhosen.'

S.b.d.

The fart employed by spies when on a mission; the *silent but deadly*. It's not true that SBDs are smellier than their frapping cousins, but they are a much less *gentlemanly* way to conduct your anal affairs. A loud noise is considered a polite warning of the stench soon to come.

SBD farts usually lead to the '*whoever smelt it dealt it*' method of apportioning blame.

See also: whoever smelt it dealt it

school dinners are cool dinners

A much-maligned effort to encourage children to eat school dinners in the mid-90s was the 'School Dinners Are Cool Dinners' advertising regime. This was just one example of the many hundreds of times that the fact that 'school' rhymes with 'cool' failed to make school any cooler.

school medical Lies have long abounded about the details of the school medical, stories of sexual abuse being little more than early claims to have shagged a nurse, or the early stages of power-imbalance fantasies. Some have more detailed recollections than others, though:

'In junior school I had a school medical where a man made me run round the gym naked. No one believes me and thinks it's some kind of strange fantasy, but it must be true as I remember dropping a mini skip and a jump in and no one fantasises in that much detail.'

scoper The Spastics Society changed their name to Scope in a bid to stop people using the word spastic as an insult. We didn't lose a word, we gained one. And it was *scoper*.

screaming gym Imagine, if you can, a very deaf PE teacher.

Secondly, imagine that his hearing aid doesn't convey anything said to him in a high register.

Thirdly, imagine how easy it is to scream without opening your mouth very wide.

Then, imagine a school gym containing 50 adolescent boys, running around in a big circle, screaming at the top of their lungs with the teacher standing in the middle of it all, completely oblivious.

And, if you want to, you can imagine 50 boys all being put on detention when the headmaster bursts in.

seagulls, exploding As we've already established, they just don't. *See: jumping on animals*

sea of legs A gentle form of violence in which a child walking through a densely seated area may be obstructed with the legs of any seated children who can get close enough. The game, born in a bowling alley where there was fixed seating, translates well into the classroom, where the flimsiness of the chairs leads to lots of people rolling around on the floor.

A more macho incarnation is *run the gauntlet*. This differs in that the victim volunteers to avoid the legs to demonstrate his skill and agility. The other participants will trip, spit and kick as viciously as they can, hoping to cause the most serious injury in the world, which is *splitting someone's head open*.
See also: head open, he's split his

self-styled nicknames

Fans of *Red Dwarf* will know of 'Ace' Rimmer's attempts to create for himself a cool nickname. If you must try and invent yourself a nickname, remember that people don't just hand out compliments, so at least try for one that might be seen as an insult (see *log*). Your friends will not willingly call you Mad Max, or Dr Funkencool.

sergeant major

'A game played by a lot of girls behind a garden shed in our bucolic playground in primary school. My friend, who invented the game, would always be the Sergeant Major and another girl would be her Second-in-Command.

'Mostly the Second-in-Command would be played by a nice, docile girl who was kind to us, but occasionally the school bully would take that role, which would add an extra frisson to the proceedings.

'The game was very simple and involved the Sergeant Major lining up the other girls against the shed and giving out small but curiously disturbing punishments such as boob-pinching and Chinese burns if we didn't stand up straight enough. It usually lasted all lunchtime because of our lax posture. Despite the oddness this was one of our favourite games.

'My friend who played the Sergeant Major also instigated Lesbian Day every other Friday.'

sex chase

A more extreme version of kiss chase which never really took off, what with the connotations of serious sexual assault.

sex education

- **Vagina**: Male teachers – if your class is giggling at the word vagina, don't say, *'Well, you wouldn't make very good doctors, would you – what would you do if I came into your surgery and said, "Doctor, there's something wrong with my vagina"?'*

- **Homosexuality**: In times of Clause 28, it was perfectly acceptable for teachers to refuse to talk about what gays did on the grounds that *'it is disgusting'*. The best way to deal with this response is to ask again.

- **Biology**: 'Everybody draw an organ of the body. Choose sexual organs if you like. Do you want to draw a penis, David? It's perfectly all right if you do.' Whether this was reverse psychology or simple eeriness was never quite worked out, but he got his penis. Oh, yes. He got his penis.

- **Openness & Expression**: 'To encourage us to be open about the body, we drew around a child on the floor, and were invited to write down slang names for all the parts of the body on it. After initial reluctance, the class quickly dissolved in a tsunami of filth.'

sexy sue

The gayest boy in the class is Sexy Sue. It is Sexy Sue's task to run around, trying to grab the penises of the other boys. However, you can defend yourself by hitting Sexy Sue. Pre-emptive strikes are allowed and encouraged.

shagging a tree

'One person would be elected the "puller" and the rest of us would grab hold of the tree trunk for dear life. The puller would attempt to remove pupils one by one from holding on to the tree by sheer force and if you were removed, you became a second puller and were then employed in removing others from the tree. The winner was the last one to be left clinging on to the tree.

'This game, however, died a rapid death after some of the older boys said we all looked like we were trying to shag the tree. It did, too.'

Shame! Mock any embarrassing situation with the word '*shaaaaaaame!*', followed by a stroking of the chin between thumb and forefinger.

Regional variations: '*Shamola!*', where you rub the forefingers of either hand together, and oddly enough, in Wellington, saying 'TAAAAAAAAY!' and pulling a lower eyelid down.

Shame! can be accompanied by licking the finger and holding it to the shamed person's face. The heat of their embarrassment will cause the spit to '*sizzle*'. Well, it won't, of course – that's why you have to shout '*sizzle*'.

Sharpe ball 'A game of throwing a screwed-up paper ball around the class, originally played in the classroom of Mr Sharpe. *Sharpe Ball* was so enjoyable that it was adapted for lessons without Mr Sharpe, by pushing drawing pins into the paper, which caused some bleeding when thrown hard.'

Shat poo The funniest thing that can be left by scratching away the letters of 'Shatterproof' on your neighbour's ruler.

Shat poof The second funniest thing.

Sherbet snorting Like smoking dried bananas, one of the many things you can do as a child that won't get you high, apart perhaps from the release of adrenaline that comes with extreme pain.

The procedure would usually be to pour, chop, snort and then bellow as loud as possible to indicate the strength and status of your 'high'. With a particularly fat line, sherbet-activated mucus foam would pour from your nose, covering yourself and those near you.

Shit sticks An offshoot of graffiti art, thought to originate in schools around Leicester. Often using twigs or lollipop sticks, urban artists would find fresh dog shit and thrust the sticks into the poo.

What remained was both a work of art, and an Excalibur-style weapon for a brave child to withdraw and wave around threateningly. Such a brave child had to be very careful of the 'double dipper'.

See also: poo on a stick

shite hawk
A game loosely based on 'Street Hawk', TV's motorbike *Knight Rider*. The rules: after school, someone's little brother would ride around the playground on his BMX as close to 200mph as he could get, while the older boys threw rocks at the wheels.

showaddywaddy
The nickname for polyester wadding which was one of the two major materials we used for making everything in first year textiles. The irresistible pleasure of saying 'showaddywaddy' throughout every textiles lesson made the teacher so angry that the classic punishment of 2,000 lines was handed out. Before the printing of this book, this has to be the most times that 'polyester wadding is not a popular music group' has been written down.

sidney homes
A summer game. When the grass has grown, choose an area of ground for your *Sidney Home*. Gather some friends (or people who like spitting) and get them to hack up a load of greenies on to the plot. Cover this with ripped-up grass and repeat. Once you are happy with your home, and have enough friends to feel safe, throw someone weak on to his new *Sidney Home*.

Other municipal features may make the *Sidney Home* even more desirable, as featured in the illustration, overleaf.

sidney towers
A *Sidney Home* with more than five floors.

silence in the courtyards
Silence in the courtyards,
Silence in the streets.
The biggest gob in England,
Is just about to speak.
Starting from ... NOW!

Often used in classrooms as a teacher approaches, or in shared rooms to shut people up and allow sleep. In some versions of this game, however, sound effects are allowed, as long as they don't form words. So those attempting to sleep will be kept awake by cacophonic grunting.

Sidney Homes

1. The basic Sidney Home. This is the bare minimum required for a Sidney Estate.

2. Municipal Dogshit. You might like to find a dogshit and use it as a community focus for your Sidney Town planning.

3. Sidney Lido. A puddle of fleg without the hassle of a grass topping, the Lido guarantees a moist patch for any visitors.

4. Sidney Towers. The bustling heart of larger estater. An area of much grass and many bogeys.

5. Community Anthill. A rare but exciting addition to any Sidney Estate.

Remember also that the phrase *biggest gob* can easily be replaced with many other choice expressions. Such as *biggest fattest anus*, or *shittiest knickered pikey*.

silver burdett 'Series of music books, filled with retarded songs that kids were meant to sing instead of hymns during assembly in our Godless primary school. The only tunes I can remember are:

Jiggle jiggle jiggle jiggle,
Jiggle jiggle jiggle,
Little sack o' sugar
I could eat you up.

And: I went down to a party,
It was me and Ben and Mack,
And before I knew what happened,
I got an itching on my back,
Scratch, scratch my back.

'Sure, the music was safe from the oppressive spectre of religion, but boy*howdy* did it suck. Why couldn't I have gone to a Catholic school? Knee socks, kilts, fabulous stained glass and gigantic gold bleeding Jesuses. And nuns. Nuns are cool.'

sing hosanna to the King ... of Kings ... An assembly hymn with a catchy tune and a booby trap.

Sing Hosanna, Sing Hosanna,
Sing Hosanna to the King of Kings.
Sing Hosanna, Sing Hosanna,
Sing Hosanna to the King.

There is *always* someone in the hall who accidentally sings '... of Kings ...' in a faltering voice at the end of this chorus.

In one school, a slightly thick girl called Susan thought it was called 'Sing Susannah', and was therefore about her. Like anyone would go up to a King – let alone the King of Kings – and just sing her name. Then shuffle off awkwardly, realising that they hadn't planned anything else to say. Just 'Susannah'. Like anyone would do *that*, Susan. You idiot.

six-inch rule Pupils of opposite sexes were required, by this ridiculous rule, to remain no less than six inches apart whilst on the school's premises. Frequent were the boasts of male pupils that they could get intimate with

their girlfriends, whilst remaining six inches apart, as they were 'hung like a donkey'.

By this argument, penises must have been exempt from the rule, which is a *glaring* loophole in a rule against intimacy.

Skid marks

Bunching can cause skid marks, as can receiving a *wedgie*. Anyone wearing brown Y-fronts will be deemed to have skidded the entirety of their pants. Yellow piping around the legs is understood to be a migrated skid.

Skids are one reason why children should be taught to wipe their arses by a professional, and not left to pick up all the bad habits of their parents.

Skid tracks

Areas of compacted snow used for highly territorial skidding. What *polyvelts* were made for. Note the difference between skid marks and skid tracks. It might save your life. **See also: polyvelts**

Skil / Skill

Skil is pronounced the same as *skill*, but it doesn't mean the same thing. We have found that *skil* has many meanings.

1. An African Bum Disease.
2. Spastic Kid In Lesbo-Land.
3. A spot on a dog's anus.
4. Dolphin or penguin shit.
5. Any of a miscellaneous list of bummers' diseases.

The most commonly known meaning of *skil* is an African Bum Disease, which led to this everyday conversation:

A: Have you got skil?
B: Yes.
A: But aha! Skil is an African Bum Disease.
B: No, I've got the skill that's in the dictionary.
A: Yeah, the African medical dictionary.

In extreme cases of *skill*, the surname McGill may be added.

Skoda mode

From that bizarre period in the late 80s when the mere hint of the word 'Skoda' could cause paroxysms of laughter, especially from a Phil Cool or Jasper Carrott studio audience.

To taunt someone whose parents

drove a Skoda, everyone would run around as fast as possible, until somebody shouted 'Skoda mode', at which point you all stopped dead.

It was a dark period for satire.

Slogs The beatings delivered to a person who has just farted. The only way to stop the slogs (short of waiting for your beaters to become bored) is to recite the alphabet, forwards then backwards, then naming three teachers. Shouting 'no slogs' immediately after farting offered some defence, but not if you were unpopular.

Beware saying 'no slogs' in case another person says it at the same time and 'jinxes' you. You will then be left in the difficult position of possibly being slogged, and unable to protest that you had actually said 'no slogs', because that would be talking whilst jinxed, and you'd get slogged. *See also: jinx*

Slow clapping, attempted disruptions to Any teacher trying to disrupt the slow clapping of an unpopular pupil's award ceremony by clapping faster than everyone else is doomed only to add a jazzy off-beat to the taunt, which will be enjoyed by all.

Sly fox Gobbing on the back of one's hand and flicking it on to the back of a teacher.

Sly old fox More insults from the sputtering mode of rage, where the mist prevents the victim from forming proper, angry insults. In this mode, watch out for insults like 'you're nothing but a sly old fox', and maybe 'you big bagpuss'.
See also: egg dribble, emery dermis

Smell my cheese 'Smell my cheese,' the bully would invite. Cheese famously smelling delicious, you would eagerly bend over to the waiting fist, anxious to see if there is a tiny cube of fragrant cheese concealed within. As you get closer, you become suspicious. There's no cheese here ... and then, the bully would punch you in the nose. A nice touch is when the bully feigns offence, and

says, 'Smell my cheese, would you?' and walks off as though you've just committed the grossest breach of cheese-sniffing etiquette.
See also: you just drank my wee

smell yer ma Usually followed by a five-second fist-fight.

... smells As in this conversation between Simon and Duncan:
Duncan: Simon ...
Simon: What?
Duncan: ... smells.

smelly telly 'The remarkably immature outburst of one history teacher when anyone mentioned television. There we would be, sagely discussing the journalistic merits of the *Equinox* programme, and he would pop up and shrill "*smelly telly!*" in our faces. We rolled our eyes indulgently.'

snorkel **1.** A Parka jacket with the hood fully zipped, creating a snorkel effect. **2.** Diving apparatus. 'When one child in our school was killed in a road accident whilst wearing her Parka fully zipped up, at assembly we were warned of the danger of crossing the road wearing a snorkel. The image of a girl crossing the road in full diving gear caused just enough laughter to get the whole year put in detention.'

soapy A name for those whose foreskins are too tight to achieve a painless erection. To loosen the foreskin, doctors advise masturbation with soap and water. To be called soapy, therefore, you have told people that you have a tight foreskin, that you have been to the doctors with your tight foreskin and that the doctor has prescribed you a course of soapy wanks. If you get ridiculed, you can hardly be surprised.

soapy tit wank When asked whether you've had sex, you may reply, 'I've had better than that.' Your pubescent peers will be aghast; what is better than sex? Sex is all there *is*. There will be an excited clamour. Before too long, nod sagely and say, 'I had a *soapy tit wank*.'
The kudos is unimaginable.

softest punch, the A simple ruse. Suggest a competition to see who can hit the other person the softest. Allow the victim to go first. After he has lightly tapped you on the shoulder, you let him have it with a perfect dead-arm, before informing him that he has won.

Warning: This trick is EMINENTLY REVERSIBLE. It is probably wise to ask if your friend has ever played 'softest punch' before. And for God's sake, remember – *they get the first punch.*

soggy biscuit A game that has all the hallmarks of a legendary urban myth. People know about it, and you're always two handshakes (the safest distance) away from someone who claims to have played it. You never meet anyone who directly claims to have played the game. However, when a survey was carried out amongst 1,866 men, the results were surprising.

The 190 people who chose 'Other' must have been people who have refereed a game, or provided the biscuit. *See illustration overleaf.*

soggy boggies Glaswegian name for wet toilet roll, thrown on to the roof or wall to lend it a stippled 3D effect. Once dried, new layers can be applied, until the room is so thick with soggy boggies that you can barely get in.

Soggy boggies are also effective as a non-lethal short-range weapon.

soup The damp build-up of sweat that forms in the arse crack of Farah-wearing post-pubic boys sitting on plastic chairs in hot summer classrooms.
'Soup, Watson?'
'Certainly, Holmes, a possible broth if this heat carries on.'

space invaders A game which requires steps, a football and several young children so eager to play with the big boys that they are willing to approach very slowly down some steps towards young men, who are kicking footballs at them.

The younger boys start on the top step, chanting *'we are space invaders'*. Once hit by a football, a space invader moves on to the next step down – an

28.7%

19.6%

35.3%

10.2%

6.2%

1866 men were asked: How close have you got to the game of Soggy Biscuit, in which you race to wank onto a cracker?

28.7%: I've never heard of it.
35.3%: Never played it – I think it's a myth.
19.6%: I've never played it, but I know someone who has.
6.2%: I've played it.
10.2%: Other.

improvisation from the strict format of the arcade game, allowing for more bruises. Now you must run faster, and say '*we are space invaders*' more loudly. Once you reach the ground floor, by which point you should be sprinting and *screaming* 'we are space invaders', you are allowed to move to the top step again.

There was always a queue to play *space invaders*. No one ever really thought to stand aside and simply watch. Apart from the bemused teachers.

spam A slap to the forehead.

The counter – holding a guarding hand over the forehead – led to the development of neckback, or *maps* – a slap to the back of the neck, or head.

This, in turn, led to the invention of a double guard, which resembled hiding under your arms. To counter this defence, the aggressors invented the 'lipblap'. This involved slapping down at a person's mouth (when they were talking, for best effect), causing them to look and sound stupid and make a wet blubber noise.

So, there was always one route of attack open to the dedicated, although the quick choices to be made by the attacker and the guarder usually resulted in a simple face punch.

spazmoid Is to spazmo as cuboid is to cube. That is to say, some of the sides are of different lengths, but every face is a rectangle ... only ... with spazmos.

speednob *Speednob* involved drawing as many penises as possible on a colleague's text book/exercise book/ bag/homework diary/piece of artwork/ photograph of dead relative, and so forth, whilst their back was turned. It was perfected to three loops, removing pen from paper only to draw in a 'T' at the top. Twenty nobs in ten seconds was a skilled, but not uncommon, occurrence.

Most effective when employed on a borrowed book, swiftly drawn while the classmate is looking away, or drawn across a piece of work that your classmate is about to hand in. There are no hard-and-fast rules for drawing the cock, but in most illustrations the cock is circumcised and the balls look like two croquet hoops with three hairs each.

Speednob led to *chunderbunder*. An identical nob motif, but with one important and dangerous difference. The addition of an eye was accomplished by stabbing a biro as hard as possible into the exercise book, ideally penetrating 20 or more pages and providing a lasting reminder of the attack. Victims of a *chunderbunder* had to be careful when defending to avoid a stab wound in the hand.

speednob, advanced

Speednob became such an obsession in some schools that it was unusual to see any ink-permeable surface without a nob on it. Eventually pupils were so alert to preventing their property being speednobbed that it was very difficult for even the most committed player to nob anything at all. The only option for the potential artist was to draw a nob on an eraser, then stamp the targeted item. This marked a new era of speednob efficiency.

Note: An idiot's variant is to draw the nob on your own thumb, and use that as a stamp. Spending the rest of the lesson wiping an ink cock of your own making off your thumb is not worth it.

speednob, monster

A coastal race against time. Children on the beach must draw a 300-foot long detailed phallus in the wet sand, before teachers can descend a cliff to stop you.

Chances are, however, that the teachers will simply look dismayed and let you have your fun. Which is pretty patronising, when you think about it.

speednob reversal
See: normans

spit climbing

Little gifts left on branches to make climbing a tree more difficult and unpleasant for those who follow you. These can include regular spit, greened spit and the impassable chewed-up soggy cheese and onion crisps.

spitfire nose cones
See also: dead heat in a zeppelin race; two ferrets fighting in a sack; two bald men (but not in this dictionary you won't)

spitting in someone's mouth
A heartwarming story from a deranged child. The spelling remains unchanged, as it offers a bonus insight into wrong minds:

'This is great fun, we normally did it to cunt kids with big chins, we used to get them on the ground then we got a group of people to spit in his mouth then started poking at his face saying "HAHAHA you now have AIDS you have technolcally kissed loads of males you willy wufter" then kicked them in the face for old time sakes.'

splogger
A game combining the intellectual with the violent. It involved two teams of boys, each having a word made up of as many letters as there were team members. Each member was then given a letter. To guess the word, the other team had to extract the letters by any means necessary. Once everyone's been punched into submission, it's just a simple matter of rearranging the letters, or carrying on punching them until they just tell you the damn word.

splogger, dirty
The rules are the same as *splogger*, only there is one team of boys and one team of girls. And instead of violence, the opposing team has to be as intimate as possible, until you become hysterical with embarrassment.

Dirty splogger lasts much longer, and involved more children putting their hands behind their heads and going 'aaah'.

spoon
A unit of activity or hard work. When a classmate exerts more than the accepted 'minimum effort' in the classroom, mime the motion of spooning a substance out of a container. This substance is 'effort' – feel free to say 'eff-*ort*' whilst spooning.

For extreme cases, mime a mechanical digger shifting tons of ef*fort* at a time. Watch out for putting too much effort into your mimes, though.

Spooner A male born with no kind of genitals whatsoever. Possibly, we have decided, based on the resemblance of the bare groin to the smooth, featureless ... shiny ... back of a spoon. This may be based on the sexless but affectionate practice of spooning; presumably, anyone choosing to simply *hug* their partner in bed rather than having sex for eight hours must be some kind of cockless neuter.

Sport billy Children who excelled at sport. The derision with which this name was delivered justified the sloth of hundreds of fat kids who had just got a Commodore 64 and didn't really want to be running around, having stitches and coughing up blood.

Squash and weights The ideal games option, held in a local sports centre.

The loud macho lads could demonstrate their iron-pumping skills in the gym while we pale anaemics hid behind the upper stairwell above the squash courts.

If caught and forced to enter the weights room, standard procedure was to occupy the exercise bike, strategically positioned behind an archway so that its user could minimise legwork and sneers from the lads, while watching Annie Lennox on MTV on the opposite wall.

Squitsies A defence to the lurgy. Girls' squitsies were performed by crossing your two forefingers, and boys do squitsies by putting their thumb between their forefingers. In lurgy hot-spots, it became common to adopt squitsies as the relaxed position of your hand, affording 24-hour lurgy protection and occasional cramping.

Steel ruler Basic tool of the classroom, devourer of fingernails.

Steptoe face, please Upon being asked, '*Steptoe face, please,*' the target had to make a face like Albert Steptoe from *Steptoe and Son*. This polite request could come at any time, even when you were in the middle of answering a teacher's question. If the required face was not made, the person making the request was entitled to beat the target up.

Stevo 'The surname Stevenson is shortened to Stevo, relengthened to Steve Ovett, Garfield's vet is called Liz, short for Lizard, the aliens were lizards in V, VD, D-Day, Day of the Dead. Therefore, Stevo, you're dead. So there.'

Stinger A circumcised child. Named after the fact that cutting your foreskin off must fucking sting.
See also: b.t.

Stop the bus and eat a wee-wee 'My favourite school bus song was "*Stop the bus and eat a wee wee*". I loved it so much; it was so funny that people would eat a wee-wee at all, let alone stop an entire bus to do so. My hysterical reaction would often

result in worried looks from fellow passengers. Much the same look, in fact, that I received when telling this story to my boyfriend. He rather furtively suggested that perhaps I'd misheard the words: "*Stop the bus I need a wee wee.*" Oh, the shame – the retrospective shame.'

Incidentally, the final line of 'and the boys at the back can't swim' clearly overestimates the capacity of the human bladder and the urine-tightness of the average bus.

Street Survey Pointless time-filling geography exercise, compulsory for every child in Britain to perform at least once. It involved writing down the registration plate of every car in the chosen street, and perhaps writing down how many red cars went down the new road in 10 minutes.

The sheer pointlessness of this exercise was compounded by the fact that they never chose stretches of road anywhere near fag shops.

stretch armstrong

Game for two or four players. Requires one Armstrong. Split into two teams and pull on alternate sides of the Armstrong, until the Armstrong is stretched, or broken.

stuck in the mud

Variation of *tig* (also *tag*, *dobby*), where the person who's been *tigged* (also *tagged*, *dobbed*) has to stand still and can only be freed by having someone crawl through their legs. The only reason anyone would risk their own mobility by attempting this is (a) if they are your friend, (b) if they are desperately unpopular and think maybe that you will thank them for it later, or (c) if the bristle of thigh against shoulder is something of a thrill to them.

Once a player was *stuck in the mud*, you could dive violently into the back of unpopular people's legs and send them sprawling to the floor. Being technically still paralysed, they would have to rise to their feet and remain still, allowing you to do it again. And again.

Suck my ...

Verbal trap. Asking a victim if he wanted something, you would then deny him with a rhyme:

> *Do you want a sweet?*
> *Yes, please.*
> *Suck my feet! Do you want some jelly?*
> *All right then ...*
> *Suck my belly! Do you want a hat?*
> *Not really.*
> *Suck my cat! Do you want a punch?*
> *Look, no. No, I don't. Shut up.*
> *Eat my lunch!*
> *Fuck off.*

Sugar solution

When you first start chemistry lessons you cannot be trusted with real chemicals in case you hurt yourself or throw them in someone's face.

Hence, 'litmus paper' experiments with sugar solution. The fact that the paper does absolutely nothing when put in the liquid proves without doubt that it is neither acid nor alkali, but just water with sugar in it.

RESULT.

supply teachers, trans-sexual

'Our school had a run-in with a transsexual supply teacher, who took us for a lesson in "line dancing". Line dancing with a ladyboy – an integral part of the curriculum in SW London.'

swastika grid

The pastime of the third row in maths (intelligent but not geeky) was to fill in the grid provided by maths textbooks with swastikas. It wasn't so much that they were all Nazis, but that you could fit exactly 16 on a page and they looked rather pleasing. They also offended those annoying girls with liberal mums, who you couldn't even call someone gay or fat in front of.

See also: nazi chair arrangements

swear words, permitted

You may say bitch and sod, because a 'sod' is a clump of grass, and a 'bitch' is a female dog. Bastard provides an acid test, as the real meaning is actually the point of the insult.

Twat, somewhat less convincingly, can be used to mean a pregnant goldfish. This might be an insult that is in common use in Egypt, along with 'may the fleas of a thousand camels infest your armpits'. **See also: twat**

sweaty betty

The moment every classroom is exposed to The Macc Lads for the first time is a special one. For the one child who brought in the tape, or relates stories of the lyrics to a disbelieving crowd, it's a real South Park 'Asses Of Fire' moment, with children waking up to a new era of filth.

swimming, avoiding

You are going too far if you present your teachers with a bundle of lumpen, shit-filled keks as proof that you are ill. Generally, fingers down the throat or a note will suffice. Actually producing tangible turds is considered a little much.

For girls, simply say that you have your period. Beware of the teacher's trick of writing 'P' by your name, to monitor which girls are having four periods a month.

T t

ta club, the 'A club with only two members, the Doctor and the Assistant. Patients would queue up for their operations, which consisted of a sharp stab in the hand with a compass, and a blob of Tipp-Ex on the wound (for "healing"). When the operation was over you had to say "ta". Hence the name of the club.'

ta ra ra bum di ay

> *Ta ra ra bum di ay,*
> *My knickers flew away,*
> *They came back yesterday,*
> *Ta ra ra bum di ay.*

This unusual narrative casts aside the traditional form of beginning, middle, end, by leaving out the middle section that can be so *boring*. The knickers are gone – the knickers are back. However, the repetition of the first line in the last reminds us that it is a constant cycle, and no sooner have one person's knickers returned, than another pair has flown away.

tally ho! Posh and less patriotic version of British Bulldog. One person started as the 'catcher' and everyone else had to get from one side of the playing area to the other. To catch someone you had not only to dob/tag/

touch them, but to pin their shoulders to the ground by all means necessary for three seconds.

By all means necessary is perhaps melodramatic – I mean, we never used a violent armed uprising to pin someone to the ground for three seconds.

taxi In Cornwall, after you farted, you said 'Taxi' while putting your thumb on your forehead. There were no recriminations or other rules – this was really just a badge of pride in case anyone hadn't heard or smelt the guff. *Taxi translated roughly to – 'I've farted! Woo-hoo!'*

tchaikovsky

Tch-tch-tch-tch-tch-tch-tch-tchaikovskeeee;
Here he comes, banging his drums.
Whilst singing this song, stride purposefully around the playground whilst beating your chest with your fists. Tchaikovsky wasn't known for his drumming skills, so you don't have to be very good.

teacher behaviour, inappropriate
'On top of a French teacher who told us that he was "going home to beat his wife" at the end of every lesson, our English teacher was asked his opinion of gay men during the discussion of a Shakespeare play. His response of "men, women, tried 'em both, much the same" was so witheringly put that we could only stare helplessly at him.'

teacher teacher

Teacher, Teacher, I declare,
I can see your underwear.
We break up; we break down,
we don't care if the school burns down.
No more English, no more French,
no more sitting on the old school bench.
Teacher, Teacher, I declare,
I can see your underwear.
Is it black or is it white,
or is it made of dynamite?
This song dates back many decades, and stays true to the theme of children getting to the last line and just not bothering any more. Underwear made out of dynamite, apart from being dangerous,

would be impractical and uncomfortable. Of *course* the teacher's underwear isn't made out of dynamite. Tsk.

teashop

A primitive accountancy/ risk assessment program/game.

You were the owner of a teashop, and accordingly supplied tea, using your shop. You decided the number of cups to be sold, and the price.

Things usually went smoothly, but every so often it would emerge that 'a swarm of wasps drove everybody away!' and you would howl and gnash your teeth as your empire crumbled, and 15 minutes of your childhood was frittered away in the darkest futility.

There was no option to buy wasp repellent, or to open a shop that sold wasp repellent instead of tea. A shame – with all the tea shops and wasps in the area, you'd have made a killing.

teddy bears picnic

If you go down in the woods today,
you're sure of a big surprise.
If you go down in the woods today,
you'd better just close your eyes.

Cos Mum and Dad are 'avin a shag,
and Uncle Bob is suckin' his nob,
and Auntie Mary's 'avin' it off with
Graaaandad.

Uncle Bob was probably sucking his own nob, what with it being the only one not occupied with Auntie Mary or your mum. Or he might be fluffing Grandad.

The Wallington Variation:
'Cos Uncle Ross is having a toss, and
Uncle Frank is having a wank
And Auntie Flo is having a go with
Gran-dad!

Other possibilities include *Uncle Jim having a rim*, *Aunt Irene flicking her bean*, and *Diana Rigg having a frig*. You could also have *Auntie Sue doing a poo* while *Uncle Jim kissed her quim*. Presumably Sue and Jim are German.

tefal, tefal head

An insult for children with large foreheads based on characters from Tefal adverts. These characters were scientists, and so brainy that their heads went up a foot higher than a usual head.

At breaktimes the cry 'TEFAL!' would

go up, and everyone within hearing distance would tear after some shiny-headed first year. When he was finally pinned in a corner, his forehead was measured with a ruler and the surrounding mob would chant 'TEFAL! TEFAL! TEFAL!' until breaktime finished.

telephone Pop group featured in the Longman's Audio Visual French books.

Jean-Paul et Claudette would purchase *'le dernier disque de Telephone'* every damn Saturday, without fail. If they really wanted to live life on the edge, they went swimming afterwards.

telling I don't like you and I am going to report your (real, made-up, or neither) bad behaviour to the teacher who likes me best and you least. Ha ha. I'm *telling* of you.

In cases of genuine *badness* your mouth would drop open, your eyes would widen and the only word you would be able to summon was a breathless 'tell-ing', before you ran off in a random direction until you hit something.

Telling can also be used as an effec-tive bullying device. Tell someone younger or smaller than yourself that you are 'telling on them', despite the fact that they have done nothing wrong, and they will royally cack their pants and begin to stutter the word 'but' around 20 times before hiding.

This technique is also its own defence; simply scream *'telling'* just as loudly, and start a race to the nearest teacher. Of course, if you make it to the teacher you'll have to make something up pretty quickly, or admit that you were both running around screaming *'telling'*.

telling, with reasons If *'telling'* is said with a musical lilt, then you must ask why. The person who is telling then has to tell you why. Any reason that rhymes is adequate, for example:

- Because you jumped on a lorry and you didn't say sorry;
- Because you walked in the garden and you didn't say pardon;
- Because you jumped in the pond and kissed James Bond;

- Because you went to the toilet, and when you pulled the chain, out came a great big choo-choo train.

As if Bond would be seen dead in your crappy pond.

ten pence A game where one friend presses a pre-licked coin on to another friend's forehead and encourages him to dislodge it by whacking himself on the back of the head.

But the coin is really in the first friend's hand, you see, not stuck to the forehead, so the second friend is left slapping the back of his head in vain, resembling the late Eric Morecambe in a state of arousal.

See also: glass eye

ten per cent exam bet A bet in which the participant to score closest to 10% on an important exam *without going under* wins.

Patently open to abuse by the '*You didn't really try to get 10%, did you? Christ, it was only a joke and now you've thrown your future out of the window*' brigade.

terrence trent d'arby Terrence is a gay name. The River Trent runs through Nottingham. Derbyshire is a neighbouring county to Nottinghamshire, where the locals fuck trees, cows and sisters. Terrence Trent D'Arby is therefore quite a potent insult, meaning that you live in a river, are gay, and fuck trees, cows and your sister.

tesco conga Where Trevor buys his best clothes. The more people in the conga line, the truer the song will seem.

Let's all go to Tesco's,
Where Trevor buys his best clothes,
They are so nif-TY!
For one pound fif-TY!

testicular pursuit You will *need*: sunlight, a watch.

The object: to reflect sunlight from your watch on to the testicles of the unsuspecting teacher. If he is wearing clothes, aim at the crotch of his trousers.

The beam is diverted away from the teacher once he has begun to suspect that the entire class is laughing at his nob. Conceivably, if everyone in the class did the same thing, you could set the teacher's trousers on fire. In larger classes on planets closer to the sun, you could sear through the testicles like a laser.

that's not my leg Write

clearly on your leg 'Not my leg'. When somebody asks you why you've got that written on your leg, you simply reply, 'That's not my leg.'

that's what your mum said to me in bed last night A put-down that doesn't

really require you to listen to the other person's comment. Unless the person you are speaking to has just said, 'Oh, it's a baby earthworm sleeping on a couple of hairy pebbles.'

the bells, the bells The

yanking of, and sometimes swinging from, a fellow student's tie until the knot is irreversibly wee. This is also known as a 'peanut', and only becomes

a 'the bells, the bells' if you say so, in Quasimodo's voice.

the earth is yours o god

The one opportunity you will get to shout 'shit' during an assembly.

'*The Earth is yours O God, You nouriSH IT with rain.*'

three holes A misconception

about the female body.

'When told that there were "three holes to choose from" when having sex with a girl, I interpreted this to mean that women had three vaginas, and the important thing to learn was which vagina to penetrate. I had no idea what would happen if you got the wrong one, but I imagined it was like something out of *Indiana Jones*, with poisoned arrows flying into your cock or something.'

three men on a stroll

Inform a friend, on the way to swimming lessons, that you have a fascinating story for him and could you please just see his hand?

Procure a pen and draw three tiny

stick figures on top of his hand. Tell him: 'There were three men having a walk. One was blind, one was dumb and one was deaf. Here goes the blind one (draw the man's path up the victim's arm); tell him when to stop.'

Break off the line when your friend says stop.

'Here goes the dumb one. Tell him when to stop.'

Same thing again.

'Here goes the deaf one. Tell him when to stop.' Your friend will do so. Only this time, just carry on drawing for as long as you can. The man's deaf, you see. He can't hear you.

You don't have to be on the way to swimming lessons, but the man *must* be deaf.

tie cracker Entertainment while waiting for fat kids to get dressed after games. Ties would be wrapped around the hand and cracked, sometimes very loudly, like whips.

This was because the tip was travelling faster than the speed of sound, like a jet engine.

ties 'At my school, there was a crude – yet strict – system of classification according to how you wore your school tie. A "Slim Jim" was worn by cool kids. A "Fat Twat" was sported by the geeky, swotty kids.

'Some wore both styles in a crude metaphor for the bi-polar nature of their personalities. But not many.'

ties up This can only be asked of someone who is wearing a tie and V-neck jumper: 'What does a ship do when it gets to the harbour?' The answer is, of course, 'Ties up!', which you shout while swiftly tugging their tie from behind their jumper. Only really resulted in mild irritation, but it was a popular thing to do.

One can only imagine the myriad answers gone through before the 'victim' finally says, 'Ties up.' 'Drops anchor'? Sounds a bit rude, but not the response needed. 'Lets the passengers off'? Well, yes, a ship will do that. But not a rich source of comedy. Picture the prankee's desperate hints about ropes and knots before eventually resorting to, 'Look, just say "Ties up", OK?' 'What? Oh OK, ties up. Oh look, you've lifted my tie out of my jumper. I am now mildly irritated.'

tight or loose
This test was carried out by a gang of girls waiting just inside the classroom by the door. The leading girl has a ruler. All males entering will find a ruler being poked into their genital area. Then, depending on your posture, they would should 'TIGHT' (if you curled up protectively or seemed shy), or 'LOOSE' (if you strode through manfully).

Why? The only explanation we can think of would be that striding in manfully implies that you have nothing to be ashamed of – i.e. you have a large penis – therefore you would be requiring a loose vagina. In this sense, it's not a form of feminine intimidation; it's simply a pragmatic allocation of the available vaginas.

tit chase
Like kiss chase, but the rewards were less disgusting. Simply touch the breast, and go! To a pubescent boy, this is much preferable, unless you're already having real sex and kissing with tongues. Mind, even then, you probably still enjoy touching tits more than kissing.

toilet, finding a crow in the
'If you walk into a toilet cubicle to find a dirty great fucking big crow sitting on the bowl, there are two options you can follow.

'You can back away slowly and find another cubicle, or you can shit everywhere and run screaming through the crowded dining hall with your trousers around your ankles. I chose the latter course of action.'

toilet, you just cleaned my
See illustration.
- Make a loose fist, with the thumb and forefinger hoop at the top.
- Ask a friend to put their finger into the hoop.
- Ask if they would be so kind as to wiggle their finger around for a moment.
- Inform them that they have just cleaned your toilet. With their finger.

See also: you just drank my wee

you Just Cleaned My Toilet

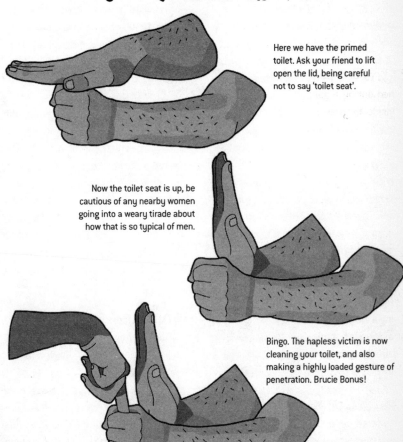

Here we have the primed toilet. Ask your friend to lift open the lid, being careful not to say 'toilet seat'.

Now the toilet seat is up, be cautious of any nearby women going into a weary tirade about how that is so typical of men.

Bingo. The hapless victim is now cleaning your toilet, and also making a highly loaded gesture of penetration. Brucie Bonus!

top gun Game named, quite obviously, after the gayest film of all time.

When the *Top Gun* craze hit these shores, the playground variant involved running around with arms outstretched to form 'wings' and their thumbs sticking out to form deadly 'guns'. To lock on to your quarry, you had to make a series of beeps. Once you were making a constant lock tone, you could fire your missile.

The only option left to your enemy would be to apply their air brakes, which they did by turning their thumbs upward. The missiles would then sail harmlessly by. Thus, no one ever got hit by the missiles, and the game degraded into physical attacks on the first person to use their air brakes.

train boy 'A kid, a couple of years our junior, who used to make the beeping noise of a train door opening, thinking it made him popular. A large group would gather round him and chant *'Go on, make the train noise!'* repeatedly. He would milk the attention for a while, prepare himself, then beep. Like a train door.

'A hushed silence would descend until he had finished. It would then go one of two ways – we would make him do it again or we would disperse, satisfied that we had just successfully encouraged a boy to beep.'

trannies Old-speak for transistor radios.

'Our friend Matt, pissed off at having his radio confiscated, was berated by the confiscating teacher, who told him that it "was his own fault for bringing a trannie into school". The rest of the day involved sketching Matt with a hairy bloke in stockings saying, "Why can't I come to school with you, Matt? Are you ashamed of me?"'

transform-a-snack race For the child who is intensely competitive but too fat to play sport, there is the Transform-A-Snack race. Packets cost 10p a bag, and up to three bags can be used in any one race. The game is played while walking rapidly and an adjudicator is required to apply improvised penalties should a crisp fall on the floor. Conceivably, more than three bags could be used, but after three bags of rapidly eaten Transform-A-Snacks, the roof of your mouth is painfully tattered, and it becomes a test of endurance rather than speed.

trebor mints Trebor Mints are a minty bit stronger. Stick them up your bum and they last a bit longer.

trevor Trevor is the standard name by which tramps are known, because they both begin with the letters 'Tr'. Add the surname of the person you are insulting for a highly personalised Trevor insult. For example, if you are insulting Chris Holmes: 'Ooww, Trevor Holmes, can't afford no food, lives in a skip, Trevor Holmes.'

triangle Musical instrument pitched at the ungifted. One step up from the wood block. Conceivably just as boring, the only fun that could be had from the triangle was by watching the clumsier members of the class set the instrument spinning with a clumsy strike on the side. Trying to stop it with their 'beater', they would end up making a loud out-of-sync ting.

tricera-tit The third nipple, or nuggie, can be termed a *Tricera-tit*. Females with three full-sized breasts might be sketched in workbooks by children who later go on to dress up as teddy bears and *frot* each other in Germany.

trick nuts Quite simply the coolest thing anyone could ever have. Apart from mag wheels. And the memorised code for infinite lives and level selection on Manic Miner.

tufty badge A medal for people showing pride in something relatively unimpressive.
   'Look at my picture of a house. I haven't gone over the lines once.'
   'What do you want, a Tufty Badge?'
   Also offer them an *O.B.E.*, a *biscuit*, or *a big shiny fucking medal*.

tuh! Exclamation used immediately after a teacher has said 'shhh!' to form an approximation of a rude word. This practice goes back to at *least* the 1940s.

twat **1.** A pregnant goldfish. **2.** An extreme twit. **3.** A fanny. Hur ... I just typed fanny.

twinkle twinkle

Twinkle twinkle little star,
What you say is what you are,
If you say it back to me,
You're a hairy chimpanzee.
Congratulations. You are now immune to everything.

two-ball-screwball Method of twisting the balls of other male children in order to speed their submission. Agreed best practice was to shout 'two-ball-screwball' during the twist.

Based on the then popular confection, the Screwball, which was a cone of ice cream with a ball of chewing gum in the nib. Lucky children sometimes found two balls of chewing gum, less fortunate children had their nuts twisted as they writhed on the floor.

U u

uh! you've got birdshit on your finger! What your friend shouts after you confide in him that you have birdshit on your finger. Reversible by wiping it on his coat and shouting, 'Uh! You've got birdshit on your coat!'

ummmmmmmm Yet another variant of *arrrrrrr*, only this time you could escape by shouting 'bum' while everyone is going 'ummmmmm', and before they get to say 'I'm telling on you'.

During lessons, it was a calculated gamble on what would get you into more trouble: getting told on, or shouting 'bum'.

unman, wittering, and zygo A film studied in some GCSE English literature curricula. Contained an inexplicable 10-second sex scene. None of us knew how it added to the plot or imagery of the film, although it was referenced in every student's essay. For example, *'No one was very good at maths because sir kept having sex scenes.'*

upside-down calculators

203

U UPSIDE-DOWN CALCULATORS

The classic.

Also contains 'boob'.

'Can you calculate the cost to the environment?'
You can use that if you like.

Breaking Esso's monopoly of
upside-down calculators.

Enjoyed brief popularity alongside Loadsamoney.

One for the ladies. Aw.

One for the farmers. Aw.

And this one's Shoe Bile. Aw.

In addition to the world-famous 55378008, the other words you can spell upside down are featured opposite. There's a story you can recite to get to 55378008, but to be honest — it's not that funny.

0.7734:	Hello
5318008:	Boobies
7100553:	Esso Oil
71077345:	Shell Oil
37183045:	Shoe Bile
45084518:	Bish Bosh
53450106:	Goloshes
60436034:	Hedgehog

See illustrations.

URINALS, ALTERNATING BOY-GIRL

U URINALS, ALTERNATING BOY-GIRL

urinals, alternating boy-girl A way of preventing the unpleasant proximity of boys pissing in adjoining urinals. Simply designate the urinals boy/girl/boy/girl, like grown-ups do at weddings.

Using a girl's urinal was tantamount to signing an affidavit reading 'Oo oo, I look at the willies and I done bums', and boys would hop desperately from foot to foot rather than face the disgust of using a girl's urinal.

'The fun was partially sucked out of the game when, as fourth years, we shouted at a first year using the girl's urinal, and he told us to "grow up".'

V v

vaginal blood fart 'The natural conclusion of an unattended blackboard filth escalation. Although the words get ruder, the number of people laughing at the phrase will reduce steadily as the class matures. Until *vaginal blood fart* was written on a university blackboard, and only I laughed.'

vaginas, the car-jacking of, premature exposure to Boobs are fun. Everybody wanted to see boobs. The panic scene in the classic film *Airplane*, where a topless lady briefly appears and jiggles them about for a couple of seconds, is the thinnest part on the videotapes of thousands of children who couldn't get their hands on anything more explicit.

When you *do* get hold of that more explicit tape, and you see a lady using a jack-like tool to open her furry garden *extrawide*, until it looks like a wretched mock-up of a flesh grotto ... then you will long for the days of innocent, bouncy breasts.

You can never go back.

variety sunshine coaches These coaches, famed for their cinema appeals in which Bob Hoskins would ask you to give money to an usherette, were also used for disadvantaged inner-city kids, as well as their more common association with the educationally challenged.

'We were momentarily gutted when we had to go on one, but we soon got into the spirit of things, pretending to be broken as the bus rolled through the streets of Leeds, all the way to the Lake District.'

vampirism, careers in

Vampirism became pretty cool after *The Lost Boys* was released. However, careers advisers would firmly advise against such lifestyle choices, on the grounds that vampires didn't exist and were evil. Eventually, the more dedicated night-fiends were forced to settle for filling a Panda Pops bottle with pig's blood, and kicking it around until it burst.

This game ends when the head vampire decides he wants to be a fighter pilot for the US navy and ride a motorbike instead.

vintage

From a deepening appreciation of the niceties and textures of extremely pungent farts, you may declare a vintage. The earlier the year, the smellier and more complex the fart.

'Initially, you'd be forgiven for thinking this was a 1985, but when you notice the delicate undercurrent of sulphur and raspberry, you realise that it's definitely a 1983.'

virgin exit

The words 'Emergency Exit' at the back of a school bus could, with careful use of a penknife, be amended to '*Virgin Exit*'. All very funny, ha ha, but the one time in five years that the bus broke down, everyone refused to use it.

When a bus company changed their signs to 'Emergency Door', there arose the opportunity of 'Virgin Loo'.

vote labour

A moment of Python-inspired theatre.

'During a German lesson, two lads appeared at the window, wearing home-made Ku Klux Klan outfits. One was the traditional white, the other an *outré* black. The white Klan member proceeded to "kill" the black Klan member with a plastic Hallowe'en axe. Then they both dropped out of sight, before popping up in front of the bemused (and probably a bit freaked-out) class with a local election "Vote Labour" sign they had nicked from a nearby garden.

They then sprinted off past the bus stop and out of sight. This incident led to a local inquiry.'

vulcan handfanny The closest you can get to a real fanny without getting close to a real fanny. *See illustrations overleaf.*

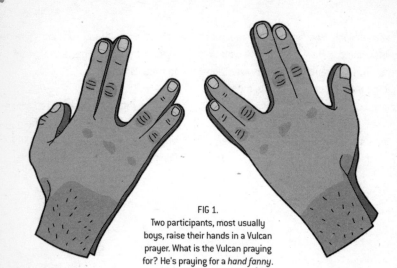

FIG 1.
Two participants, most usually
boys, raise their hands in a Vulcan
prayer. What is the Vulcan praying
for? He's praying for a *hand fanny*.

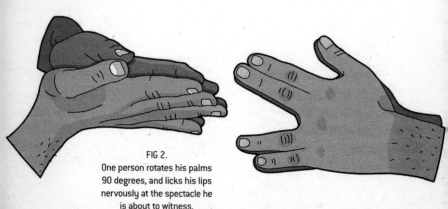

FIG 2.
One person rotates his palms
90 degrees, and licks his lips
nervously at the spectacle he
is about to witness.

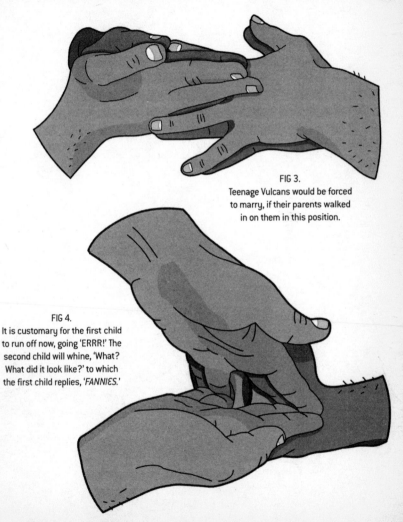

FIG 3.
Teenage Vulcans would be forced
to marry, if their parents walked
in on them in this position.

FIG 4.
It is customary for the first child
to run off now, going 'ERRR!' The
second child will whine, 'What?
What did it look like?' to which
the first child replies, *'FANNIES.'*

W w

walkers, the A process involving one victim, one person sitting on the victim's chest and two people walking in opposite directions with the victim's legs.

As a matter of non-crippling courtesy, do not walk on the victim's knees.

walking on the moon Jeer, point at and kick your victim, singing The Police song 'Walking On The Moon'. After singing for a while, the victim should be asked what it is like, walking on the moon. If they reply, 'I don't know – I've never been there,' you would plainly state, 'Yes, you have.'

wall punching A way of demonstrating how hard and/or stupid you are. It started off quite mildly but soon escalated to the stage where kids would come in to lessons with blood pouring from their knuckles.

This was tolerated by teachers and went on for some time, until the hardest/stupidest kids had the idea of using their heads instead of their fists.

wank wank oops Pretending to wank followed by flicking the wrist, and the imaginary ejaculation, to one side. As you do this, say, 'Oops!', as though ejaculating is the last thing on your mind when you're having a wank.

wank your hairy crutch

Doesn't sound anything like 'thank you very much', truth be told.

wankerchief A handkerchief set aside for exclusive wanking use. Also 'spunky wankerchief' – a freshly used wankerchief. A spunky wankerchief becomes a dirty wankerchief only when crisp. A hanky used after a single badly planned wank, and then returned to normal handkerchief duties, is not a wankerchief.

wanker's cramp Make a fist, hold it up in front of you.

'What's this?' you ask your victim.

'I don't know!' they reply.

'Wanker's cramp!' you respond, continuing with, 'Do you get it?'

'Haha! Yes!' they gleefully reply.

'You get wanker's cramp! You must be a wanker! Wanker, wanker, wanker!'

Fundamentally the same joke as 'What paper do homos read?/Don't Know./The *Gayly Mail*! Do you get it?' only this time you're a wanker, and not (necessarily) gay. Only the very gullible – or honest – will admit to suffering from wanker's cramp after reading the *Gayly Mail*.

wanking, alleged ill effects of

- *Makes You Blind*: This is bad, as you need your eyes to look at pornography and get spunk out in under a minute. 'Thinky wanks', where you close your eyes, and have to imagine tits or cocks, take much longer and are not worth it. With eyes-closed thinky wanks, you also run the risk of your mother coming in and putting a cup of tea down beside you. *See: classical wank*

- *Makes You Deaf*: 'Wa-ka Maya Deh!'
  'Pardon?'
  'Wan Kamakya Deeeh!'
  'What?'
  'Wanking Makes You Deaf!'

- *Makes Your Balls Shrink*: 'Another reported ill effect of wanking is that it uses up bits of your balls, which shrink with every toss. When they finally disappeared, you would be unable to support life, and would therefore die. Rather than making me relish each wank, this made me frantically wank at every opportunity, using the same logic that convinces fat people that eating things quickly reduces the body's ability to absorb the calories.'

war conversations, typical

'I shot you.'

'I shot you back.'

'You can't shoot me back, I shot you in the face.'

'No you didn't, you missed.'

'No, I saw your eye explode.'

'No, that was a bird.'

'Oh fuck off.'

See also: everything-proof shield-piercing bullets; infinity plus one

waving at aeroplanes

Whenever an aeroplane flies over a school playground, all the kids would wave their hands frantically in the vain hope that the pilots would mistake them for stranded civilians and land to save them from their afternoon lessons.

we are lucky cows

Based on the Anchor advert in which computer-manipulated cows danced, and sang, 'We are lucky cows, we chew the cud and browse.'

Birthed a game wherein the main player is clamped to the ground and force-fed grass, whilst a crowd recreate the song.

we won the war

After declaring war on a neighbouring gang and throwing stones at them for a while, it was customary to link arms and parade around the street singing, 'We won the war, in 1964 – guess what we done, we kicked 'em up the bum.'

This, despite the fact that it was 1978, and the other gang had only left the field of battle because it was time for their tea.

we're playing army, who wants to join us?

A chant to be heard around the playground after lunch.

Those who wanted to 'join us' would link arms with the end person and join in the chant. The game Army has never been played, because it was always time to go in by the time enough people had been recruited. Even though no one knew how many people you needed to play Army, as it has never been played.

we're walking straight, get out of our way

A line of boys would link arms and march across the playground chanting, *'We're walking straight, get out of our way.'* Then they walked, their legs kicking out in front of them in a cross between the can-can and goose step. When the line gets very long, turning around is impossible and the commitment to walking straight will lead everyone into a hedge.

weak bullying of susan bailey

'I am the most pathetic bully ever. All I did was steal one epaulette off her winter coat, then put it in her pocket so I didn't get done for stealing. And call her "Susie".'

wedgie

The practice of hoisting the waistband of a victim's underwear so that the gusset rode high between the buttocks, often grinding the balls. Walking with a wedgie is known as 'chewing cheese'.

Variations include *Skidders McKenzie*, based on the *gold watches* you would gain from a severe *wedgie*.

Reverse wedgies are known as *melvins*. A particularly feared prospect was the *atomic melvin*, in which your stretchy boxer-briefs were pulled so far up that the elastic band could be placed over your head.

See also: gold watches

wee!

As a childish word, the word actually came to mean childish in some areas. Immature acts are to be met with cries of 'Wee!' As an adjective: 'God Jim, you are so wee!' Finally, as an unbeatable retort to an insult: 'Oh, *wee*.'

wee and poo

A game to be played in pre-litigation concrete playground boats. Divided by two planks of wood, one side is designated 'wee' and the other side 'poo'. The game consisted of getting someone in either half and then running around the boat shouting 'you're in poo' or 'you're in wee', as appropriate, and laughing at them.

One variation was for everyone to trot around the edge of the boat, or on the planks, trying to push each other into the wee or poo hemispheres, and *then* shouting 'wee' or 'poo' at each other.

wee tap, the 'The middle water fountain on the playground at Hillbrook Infants School dispensed pure wee. Anyone drinking from the middle fountain would have stones thrown at them, and '*wee tap*' screamed in their faces.

'On the hottest days in summer, massive queues would form for the other two taps. The wee tap was always free, if you dared ...'
See also: urinals, alternating boy-girl

well, you're not at home now Rather feeble comeback to the pupil's positive reply to the original question, 'Do you do that at home?'

were you raised in a barn? A standard example of what Bill Cosby might call *inter-generational rhetoric*.

When walking into a form room without closing the door behind you, the teacher may ask this of you. The best way out of this so far is to say, '*No, a crackhouse.*'

what's the time? Another rehearsed conversation similar to *let's-be-friends*.

Kid A : What's the time?
Kid B : Tampax nine!
Kid A : Durex-spect me to believe that?
Kid B : I johnny well do!
Kid A : Well wanks a lot.
Kid B : Tit's alright, tit's a pleasure!

A general clamour to start this exchange happened at around ten past nine every morning.

Other answers to 'What's the time?' include — if you're not wearing a watch — '*Hair past freckle*', '*Hair past skin*', or the hilarious '*Time Big Ben had babies*'. The lesser-known '*It's just gone ... so's me watch*' will assure you enduring popularity.

what you say is what you are

UK variant of *The Simpsons*-quoted classic, 'I know you are, you said you are, so what am I?' A flawed response to any insult. The planned exchange runs thusly:

Kid A: You're a gay.

Kid B: What you say is what you are.

Kid A: Touché! I am confounded.

One problem is the literal interpretation ... leading to this improbable exchange:

Kid A: You're a gay.

Kid B: What you say is what you are.

Kid A: What, I'm a you're a gay?

The more fundamental problem is that you're allowing the other person to say, 'Oh, in that case, fantastic sexy stud man train driver.' Imperfect and to be avoided.

where do you live?

Rudimentary rhyming surrealism.

Where do you live? *In a sieve.*

What street? *Pig's feet.*

What number? *Cucumber.*

Which room? *Tutankhamun.*

whisper whisper whisper whisper

You have been asked to form a line, in twos. The teacher informs you that it is necessary to be quiet, so you must whisper. Upon this decree, everyone must (audibly) whisper the words 'whisper whisper whisper whisper' to one another. The teacher would acknowledge this with a grateful 'all right, thank you'.

white board

Shoplifting permanent markers from Smiths and then substituting them for the dry wipe markers on the teacher's desk resulted in hilarity when said teacher attempted to rub off the day's notes. It was even more hilarious when one of the kids decided to play 'rude hangman' when the teacher was away for 20 minutes. When the teacher returned, he was a little surprised to find the slightly smudged word 'COC_SUC_ER' printed in large letters on the board.

who wants to join the line ... no girls!

Similar to *'We're playing Army, who wants to join us?'* but without the objective of playing *Army*, and with no girls allowed (in case of 'lurgy' infection). An utterly pointless parade, lacking even the never-achieved aim of *Army*.

who wants to play star wars ... one girl!

An amalgamation of *'We're playing Army, who wants to join us?'* and *'Who wants to join the line ... no girls!'* A tolerance towards girls (albeit strictly limited) was forced upon boys, none of whom wanted to pretend to be Princess Leia. Other than that, identical to the game of *Army*, in that we constantly said we were going to play it, but never actually did.

who's the fruity one now?

Exclamation made, à propos of nothing, by one possibly disturbed child, who leapt from his seat in the middle of film analysis class. General consensus holds that that child was, and will always be, the fruity one.

who's your new friend?

If you are late, or are moved by the teacher for your unruly behaviour, you may have to sit next to someone unpopular, or someone who smells. You will be asked who your new best friend is; both you and the smelly child must pretend not to have heard. This mutual shame will not cause a bond between the victims, and it will not be spoken of again.

whoever smelt it dealt it

The established order is:

> 'Whoever smelt it dealt it.'
> 'Whoever denied it supplied it.'
> 'Whoever made the rhyme
> committed the crime.'

This last example is often followed by, 'Aha, but that was a rhyme, so you just admitted it,' to which you may only reply, 'Bah!'

Despite some of the best minds in the world working day and night on the matter, no further possibilities have been found. These failures show the difficulties facing innovators: 'Whoever tried to tell made the smell' (inelegant); 'Whoever told the story provided the glory' (glory?); 'Whoever passed the buck gassed the truck' (only effective on trucks); 'Whoever went to the trouble to needlessly place the blame probably is responsible for the fart that started the game' (a little long).

Only known exit from this conundrum is to state 'I can't smell anything'. You can say this even if you have been arguing for some minutes about who farted, by which time it will have dissipated anyway, and the class can return to DefCon Two.

why are you doing this to me? A pitiful cry in a bullying situation that very rarely leads to a moment of quiet introspection on the part of the bully. Although it would be nice if the bully replied:

Two things really. Primarily, I'm establishing my alpha male status in the only way I know how, and having been brought up in a tough, unforgiving environment, your open bookishness and transparent physical weakness disgusts me. I may also be reacting to the rage that arises from my own domestic abuse.

More likely responses range from 'because I can', the causally challenging 'because I am', the philosophical 'because you're there', and the simple shrug of the shoulders that conveys the message 'if you have to ask why I'm doing this, you'll never truly understand'.

why have you done this to me? The instinctive cry of the RE teacher locked in a cupboard.

wide on The female equivalent of a hard on, based on the observation that when women become aroused, their legs spring open and their fanny gets wide. When a woman is 100% aroused, she will be in the splits position.

window lickers A well-known phrase descriptive of children who don't have the wherewithal to not rest their heads against the windows of their Variety Sunshine coach.

wing chun An ancient and well-regarded discipline of Kung Fu. As a close-range system of combat, spinning and high kicks do not feature heavily. As such, a shit way of impressing your friends, even disregarding the partially accurate story that it was invented by a one-armed nun.

wobble This needs to be pictured. All of a sudden, someone might touch your arm and announce 'Wobble!' whereupon everyone in your vicinity would simultaneously jump away from you, dance up and down and sing the title music to *Captain Pugwash* over and over again until you managed to touch someone else. Clearly elements of *'tig'* are involved, but the inclusion of a sea shanty is somewhat more obscure.

womble 'Our Health Education teacher pointed to a diagram of a penis on the board, and exclaimed, "The foreskin." One poor child remarked, "What's a foreskin? I haven't got a foreskin." The teacher was sympathetic, the kids less so. The teacher explained this was normal. However, when he pointed on the diagram to the testicles, only to be met by the boy's increasing confusion – "What are testicles? I haven't got any testicles" – the whole class lost all control of their senses. *Womble*, or "One-Ball", was created to celebrate this day. It turned out that he was telling the truth. It was carnage down there.'

wood doesn't conduct An unusual case of knowledge-based bullying. Using limited electrical know-how, you might be convinced that by standing on a wooden chair, you are free to stick scissors into a mains socket then turn it on. The reason you're going to be OK is because the electricity will have nowhere to go, as you are not earthed. THIS IS A LIE.

word swapping During very dull English lessons, when reading very gritty books or plays, simply swap every letter beginning with s for shit, c for cunt, b for bastard etc., etc. Simple, but with some amusing results. For instance, *Journey's End* by R. C. Sherriff is a dark insight into the life and death of First World War trench warfare. As demonstrated with such lines as 'don't shit on that bastard, it is Osbourne's cunt'.

worm patrol The philanthropic children who check the perimeter of the gravel playground for worms who have become stranded, and are in dire peril of being trodden on. Worms are picked up and delivered promptly back to sweet ploughable grass. Particularly dedicated worm patrollers may kiss the worms. This makes the worms happier.

x-ray specs A game which simply involves holding your hands up to your face in that way that makes it look like you're wearing glasses, and pretending that you can see girls' knickers. You could also claim that they had wet themselves.

From the state of childhood where the idea of seeing someone's knickers is much ruder than seeing actual genitals.

xxx movies There are a number of possible reactions to pornography:

1. Mute horror from the children who are dimly aware that they will look back fondly on their innocent days.

2. Hypnotised emotionlessness from the children who can't yet put a name to the stirrings inside.

3. Feigned pious disinterest from the soon-to-be-bullied children who put too much stock in what their parents said.

4. A curious commentary and note-taking from the sexually precocious children who're already aware that women don't wee out of their bums.

5. Mature appreciation from the children who've seen too much, too young.

6. Exaggerated vocal enjoyment from the genuinely randy or closeted homosexuals.

If the boys are alone when they see the pornography, then the above still applies, but they will also be wanking.

xylophone A variation on the *typewriter*, in which you straddle your victim's stomach, 'type' on his chest, then slap his face to return the carriage so that you can continue 'typing' on his chest for a while longer. The *xylophone* is rather more savage in that it requires four people to hold down the victim in a splayed and prone star, and as many people as fancied it are allowed to savagely beat them with maracas, kettle drum sticks, or guiros. Sometimes for as long as 10 minutes.

The practice stops when somebody passes out, wets themselves, or develops kidney damage.

Yy

yampy bats A breed of bat that runs around playgrounds, holding the skin between thumb and forefinger between their teeth, and punching people in the testicles. The only defence is to have a bat – like Batman's batsignal – drawn on your arm.

Another defence would be to hit the *yampy bat*'s jaw, causing him to bite through the skin between thumb and forefinger. This evolutionary flaw probably explains the lack of *yampy bats* in adult life.

yee ha, i'm quite gay

A teacher writes: 'An amusing sticker I found on the back of a pupil, authored and stuck there by a child who is still rightfully proud of his creation. I felt this was particularly noteworthy due to its rejoicing nature set against the subtlety and moderation of the latter part. The victim wasn't *extremely* gay, and the child had taken that into account. He was just ... quite gay.'

yemen, taking to A trip to Yemen requires the following:

1. A coat to cover the traveller's head, so that he can't see. You must then hit his head, providing a constant, reasonably gentle slapping.

2. During the slapping the travel guide informs the voyager that he is 'going to Yemen', where he must 'demand the release of Muhammad Akbar'. Meanwhile, keep saying the wise words 'Yemeny Yemeny Yemeny'.

3. Two assistants hold the coat in place while the tourist is carried around, upside down and spinning in all axes.

4. He should be left in a new and interesting place to pull the coat from his face. Wherever you left him, for the purposes of this exercise, is 'Yemen'.

Not that cruel, not painful, just baffling.

yesterday my girlfriend sucked my cock

'An instance of desk-writing, which evolved into a strange kind of soap opera. One morning, we found written on one of our desks, "Yesterday my girlfriend sucked my cock," in big black letters with a ring round it. The next day, a smaller ring had attached itself to the first, containing the words, "Today I took her from behind." The next day: "I took her from the front."

'Each day new messages were added, until the entire desk was covered. At one time, he had a brief crisis about his taste in pussies, stating, "*I like shaved pussies*", "*Actually I like hairy pussies best*", followed by the unexpectedly thoughtful, "*There are several meanings for the word pussy.*"'

you, boy!

'A fire had been started in the library during afternoon break. Mr Welch, deputy head, wasn't happy with this and called an immediate assembly in order to capture the culprit. A full half hour of shouting abuse followed from the funny little Mr Welch who got more and more angry and red in the face. We just sat there in silence until Neil asked Chris the time. Mr Welch heard this break of silence, stared at Neil and tried to shout "YOU, BOY!" while pointing at him. Unfortunately his anger took control of his legs and propelled him forward, off the stage, and into a group of frightened first years at the front of the hall. For the next year, the whole school proceeded to fall off various things, shouting "YOU, BOY!"'

you just drank my wee Your hand is a fridge. Encourage a friend to open the fridge and browse the many tiny and invisible bottles of delicious milk. Gently goad them into removing one of the bottles of milk, and drinking it. When they do, look knowing and snigger, eventually telling them that they chose the bottle that you'd weed into. The drinker would put their hand over their face in absolute horror at the prospect of drinking wee, invisible or not.

Be careful, though – if they haven't mimed a swallow, they could spit your invisible wee back into your face.
See also: toilet, you just cleaned my

you what? Person A makes a statement. You say 'You what?' They repeat the statement, and you just double it.
A: I'm just going for a shit.
B: You what?
A: I'm just going for a shit.
B: You're going for TWO shits?! JESUS!

you're bullying me Telling a bully that he is bullying you is one of the less effective ways of stopping the bullying. You are most likely to get punched for the unnecessary commentary.

The bully will not think, 'God, and bullying's wrong, isn't it?', then immediately become an architect or something. **See also: why have you done this to me?**

you're gay A whittling process, designed to prevent lower years from attempting to have any dealings with those above them.
'Excuse me but can you tell ...'
'YOU'RE GAY!'
'I'm late for class ...'
'YOU'RE GAY!'
'But I want ...'
'YOU'RE GAY!'
'But ...'
'YOU'RE GAY!'
'I ...'
'YOU'RE GAY!'

you're hard, where's your handbag? Used when someone demonstrated a fierce temper, or threatened someone, and eventually for no real reason at all.

After the victim had acted hard or tried to be tough in some way, a chorus of people would shout 'Oooooh, you're hard, where's your handbag?' and then run around with their wrists as limp as possible, mimicking the scenes of squealing, flapping and bumming that they imagined occurred in a *gay pub*.

See also: gay pub

your dad's been killed in a car crash A lie that is maintained for however long it is interesting, i.e. until the victim has cried him or herself unconscious.

your mother wears a leather wig with suede chinstraps A bizarrely popular insult for, ooh, all of one breaktime at least.

your mum The '*your mum*' game consists of luring your opponent into asking the question 'Who?', to which you respond with 'YOUR MUM!!' and are then the winner. Hours of fun.

An example in use:

'A piece of paper was thrown at the head of year. When the class was asked, "*Who threw that?*", the answer "*your mum*" came from the crowd. When the head asked who said that, the perfect reply came: "*Your dad.*"

'We spent the rest of the day entertained by the idea that the head of year's mum had come into school to throw paper at him, but had been grassed up by her own husband.'

Your mum also featured in the answers to impromptu trivia questions, such as the following:

What furry-legged insect communicates with a small dance?

Your mum.

What's the fastest land mammal?

Your mum on a bike.

What's a florin worth?

Two hand jobs and a kiss off your mum.

Z z

zen exam question A philosophy student receives his exam paper, on which the only question is: 'Is this a question?' The student strokes his chin knowingly, waits three hours, then writes, 'If this is an answer,' handing his paper in and nodding to himself. Of course, he gets an A.

No one can emphasise enough how much of a lie this is. Similarly, if you get the question, 'What is courage?', then simply writing 'This is' will not get you an A. Don't – be – stupid.

zero the hero, first the worst If you came first in a race, you could be robbed of your status as the best by the second person saying 'first the worst, second the best'.

Your only recourse in this situation is to say 'ah, zero the hero, first the worst, second the best'. The hero and the best could then argue amongst themselves about whether being a hero was better than being the best.

'Yeah, you're the best ... but you're the best of all the non-heroes.'
See also: first the worst

zocchihedron The holy grail of role-playing. The 100-sided die. Resembling a golf ball, this die was used for the percentile rolls required to hit a skeleton with a broadsword. The sides were so close together that you spent most of your time trying to work out which one was on top – and, because it was essentially ball-shaped, the fucking thing would just roll off the end of the table.

zulu roof tiles The inside of a biro pen (nib and ink), when catapulted using a standard rubber band catapult, can be made to stick in polystyrene roof tiles. Over the course of a lesson, it would look like a load of miniature Zulus had staged an assault on a Michael Caine on the ceiling, using biro pen insides.

Zulu Roof Tiles died out the very second that *Zulu Fat Kid's Arm* was invented.

zwee A creature resembling a hand walking on its five digits; a well-veined, disembodied hand with eyes. Draw the creature on any spare sheet of paper and have it say in a speech bubble, '*Zwee*'. ***See also: roger the dinosaur***

zx spectrum The computer whose owners were in direct competition with the Commodore 64. The final word: fuck off, you smelly spectrum owners, with your rubber keyboards and thermal printers that print on shiny bog roll.

We *ruled*. Commodore FORCE.